THE ACCOUNTS ASSISTANT JOB MANUAL

HOW TO DO THE REGULAR DAY TO DAY TASKS OF AN ACCOUNTS ASSISTANT IN SAGE 50

Level 33, 25 Canada Square,
Canary Wharf, London E14 5LQ
handbooks@sterlinglibs.com

www.sterlinglibs.com

All rights reserved. No part of this book may be reproduced or transmitted in any form or by any means, electronic or mechanical, including photocopying, recording or by any information storage and retrieval system, without written permission from the author, except for inclusion of brief quotations for review.

Unattributed quotations are by Sterling Libs

Copyright © 2015 by Sterling Libs

Editions ISBNs

Soft Bound	CD/Video
978-0-9931977-7-2	978-1-911037-01-9

Contents

About the Author VII

Preface – Note to the reader VIII

Warning – Disclaimer IX

SECTION 1 - GETTING STARTED – SETTING UP 1

TASK 1 - Setting the company/Business on Sage 50 Accounts 2

TASK 2 - Changing program date & setting login access rights 10
    a. Change program date 10
    b. Creating your login access rights on Sage 50 Accounts 11

TASK 3 - Dealing with nominal/Ledger codes and Tax codes 15
    a. Printing out a list of default nominal codes 15
    b. Printing out a list of tax codes 17

TASK 4 - Setting up customer records 19

TASK 5 - Setting up Supplier records 21

TASK 6 - Setting up product/service details 23
    A. Product details.. 24
    B. Defaults... 25
    C. Status... 26
    D. Ordering.. 28
    E. Sales Price... 28
    F. Stock Take... 28

TASK 7 - Setting up opening balances for ledger accounts 29
    Example: 1 – Using nominal codes 29
    Example 2: setting up opening balances using opening balances wizard in Sage. 31

SECTION 2 - PURCHASE LEDGER...33

TASK 8 - Creating a purchase order in Sage 50 Professional 34
    a. Order details.. 34
    b. Placing the order.. 37
    c. Receiving deliveries or purchase order(s) 38

TASK 9 - Processing supplier invoices and credit notes. 40
    Creating purchase invoices from your purchase orders...................................... 40
    Purchase invoice entry via batch invoice 41
    Purchase credit note entry 42

TASK 10 - Paying suppliers 45
    a. Doing payment runs.. 45
    b. Paying suppliers via supplier payment 46
    c. Printing supplier remittance 47

TASK 11 - Processing non-credit transaction payments including payroll postings 48
    Wages Posting Document 49

TASK 12 - Setting up recurring entries – standing orders & direct debits 50

TASK 13 - Dealing with petty cash transactions 53

SECTION 3 - SALES LEDGER 57

TASK 14 - Processing or recording customer invoices.. 58
    Option 1: Via customer invoices and credits tab or.. 58
    Option 2: recording invoice via customer batch invoice..................................... 59

TASK 15 - Processing customer credit notes. 60

TASK 16 - Processing customer receipts... 61

TASK 17 - Processing non customer receipts - From Cash register – Cash & Cheque 62
    Recording deposits of Cash/Cheque from the Cash register. 63

TASK 18 Processing non customer receipts - From Bank Statement – Cash/Cheque/BACs 65

SECTION 4 - DOUBLE ENTRY REVIEW 67

TASK 19 - Double entry and journals review 68
Journal Entry in Sage 50 69

TASK 20 - Reversing Journals 72

SECTION 5 RECONCILIATIONS 75

TASK 21 - VAT return preparation, reconciliation & submission to HMRC 76
a. Checklist 76
b. Select the VAT scheme & setting up e.submission credentials. 77
c. Calculate the VAT 79
d. Reconcile the figures in the VAT return above 81
e. Making adjustments to VAT return for errors in previous returns 82
f. Printing the VAT return report 84
g. Submitting a VAT Return to HMRC from Sage 50 Accounts 84
h. Correcting arithmetical errors during your VAT reconciliation process ... 87

TASK 22 - Performing Bank Reconciliation 90
i. The reconciliation process. 92
ii. Making adjustments during the reconciliation process 94

SECTION 6 - DEBTOR MANAGEMENT 97

TASK 23 - Collecting outstanding debts 98

SECTION 7 - STOCK CONTROL 101

TASK 24 - Doing stock take & posting opening and closing stock values 102
i. Doing stock take 102
ii. Posting opening and closing stock values 104

SECTION 8 - NOMINAL ERROR CHECK & CORRECTIONS 109

TASK 25 - Checking nominal ledger balances & correcting errors 110

SECTION 9 PRODUCING ACCOUNTING REPORTS 115

TASK 26 - Producing common accounting reports: 116
i. Trial balance 116
ii. Purchases day book (supplier invoices) report 118
iii. Sales ledger accounts (customer accounts), showing all transactions within the account 119
iv. Reconciled bank transaction report for the period 120
v. Audit trail report 121
vi. Profit and loss management account report. 122

SECTION 10 - DATA SECURITY 125

TASK 27 - Ensuring safety & security of accounting data 126
TASK 28 - Backing up & restoring your work 127
Backing up accounting data 127
Restoring your back up 128
TASK 29 - Checking your last processed transaction after restoring your data 132

SECTION 11 - ACCOUNTING ADMINISTRATION DUTIES 133

TASK 30 - Administrative duties you might berequired to do 134
1. Sorting incoming post 134
2. Sorting out outgoing post 135
3. Answering the telephone 135
4. Collecting outstanding debts 136

AFTERWORD 137

About the Author

Sterling Libs FCCA is the author of more than five books on the subject of practical accounting. He is a fellow of the ACCA and owns an accounting firm based in Canary Wharf, London.

Sterling is so passionate about helping young aspiring accounting professionals to better understand how accounting is done in practice and has been mentoring and training hundreds of graduates and young accounting professionals over the years.

He has championed UK practical work experience in accountancy training which has helped many individuals (ACCA students & Affiliates, AAT students, CIMA students/Affiliates, university students and graduates in accounting and also those who are already working but want more in-depth practical experience in accounting) to move their careers forward and get into employment in the UK.

Sterling is really gifted in making the complex simple and throughout his books he shows you fundamental and detailed illustrations with examples of how to perform the regular day to day tasks of an accounts assistant in a clear and concise manner using Sage 50 Accounts software. It will literally feel like he is there guiding you through every step you take in the tasks.

Check it out for yourself.

Preface – Note to the reader

Working as an accountant is a rewarding, interesting and an exciting career.

The accountancy industry is buoyant even in a difficult economic climate, and accountants enjoy a more stable career than other finance professionals.

One key factor in your national and international mobility as an accountant is your ability to demonstrate and command excellent practical work experience.

Some of the regular day to day tasks performed by an accounts assistant dealt with in this handbook include:

- *All aspects of sales and purchase ledgers and journals.*
- *Issuing and balancing petty cash*
- *processing expense claims*
- *Credit Control -Targeting Slow Payers*
- *Completing VAT returns,*
- *Performing bank reconciliation*
- *Managing petty cash transactions.*
- *Calculating and checking to make sure payments, amounts and records are correct.*
- *Stock take & stock control*
- *Producing accounting reports*

You see, accountants are needed in all areas of the economy. You are likely to be seen as a valuable core member of the finance team in any organisation with a finance department

Different sectors and employers all have their own advantages and disadvantages – you have to decide what suits your personality and career aspirations best.

This handbook will be very invaluable to you as a reference guide whilst performing your duties as an accounts assistant, bookkeeper, purchase ledger clerk or sales ledger clerk using Sage 50 accounts software.

Sterling Libs FCCA, London UK

Warning – Disclaimer

This book is designed to provide information on some of the common day to day tasks of an accounts assistant. It is sold with the understanding that the publisher and author are not engaged in rendering legal, accounting or other professional services. If legal or other expert assistance is required, the services of a competent professional should be sought.

It is not the purpose of this book to reprint all information that is otherwise available to accounting students, trainees, graduates or any other accounting professionals, but instead to complement, amplify and supplement other texts. You are urged to read all available material, learn and practice as much as possible about practical accounting and how to do related accounting roles in business and tailor the information to your individual needs.

Getting hands on practical experience in accounting is not a fast and quick thing. Anyone who decides to become competent and experienced in the duties of an accountant must expect to invest a lot of time and effort into it.

Every effort has been made to make this book as complete and accurate as possible. However, there may be mistakes, both typographical and in content. Therefore, this text should be used only as a general guide and not as the ultimate source of doing the job of an accounts assistant. Furthermore, this book contains information on day to day regular tasks of an accounts assistant using Sage 50 Accounts professional software current only up to the printing date.

The purpose of this book is to educate and entertain. The author and publisher shall have neither liability nor responsibility to any person or entity with respect to loss or damage caused, or alleged to have been caused, directly or indirectly, by the information contained in this book

If you do not wish to be bound by the above, you may return this book to the publisher for a full refund before continuing reading any further or using this book.

"Only those who have the patience to do simple things perfectly ever acquire the skill to do difficult things easily"

–*unknown author*

SECTION 1

GETTING STARTED – SETTING UP

— TASK 1 —

Setting the company/Business on Sage 50 Accounts

Here is what to do…

fig. 1

- After you double click on the Sage icon on your desk top, a 'select company' window similar to the one below will appear.

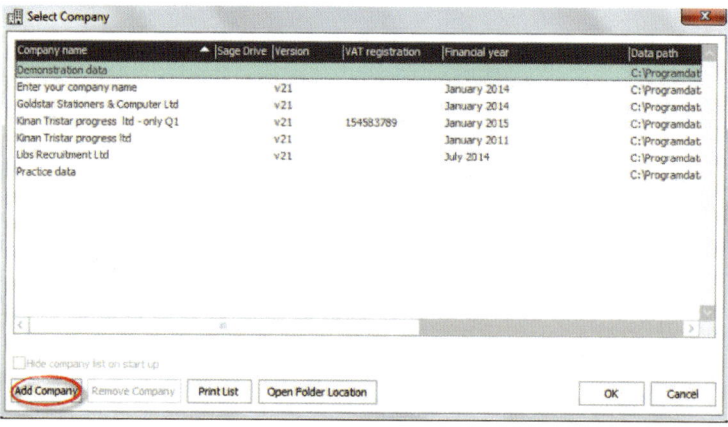

fig. 2

Click on add company – as shown in the figure above and an active setup window similar to *fig. 3* will appear

SECTION 1 – GETTING STARTED – SETTING UP

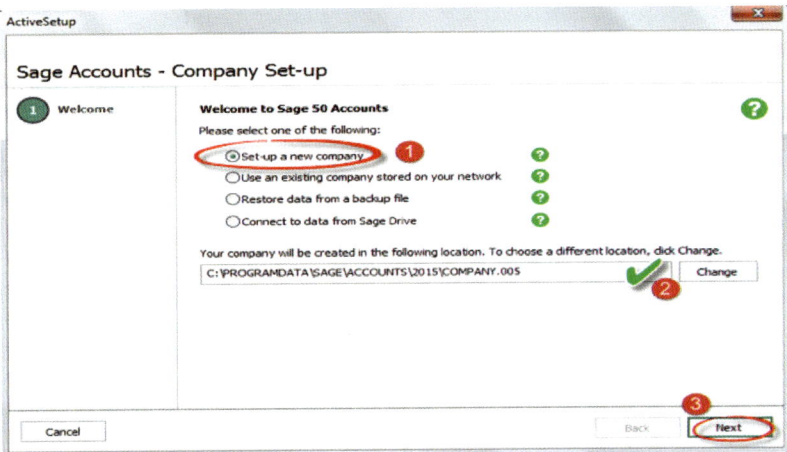

fig. 3

1. Select set-up new company

2. Select location you want to keep the new company data (to change location click change and select your preferred location)

3. Click next to continue set up

You will then see a window similar to the one below – for entering your new company details.

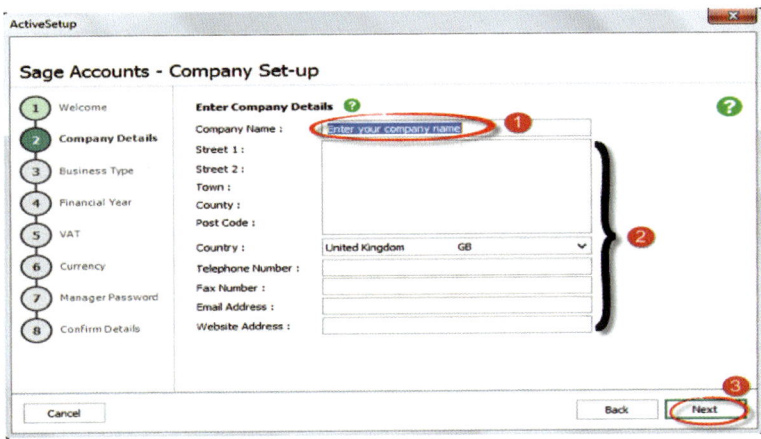

fig. 4

1. Enter your company or business name here

2. Fill up the details required here

3. Click next to continue

THE ACCOUNTS ASSISTANT JOB MANUAL

You will then see a window similar to the one below; asking you to select the business type.

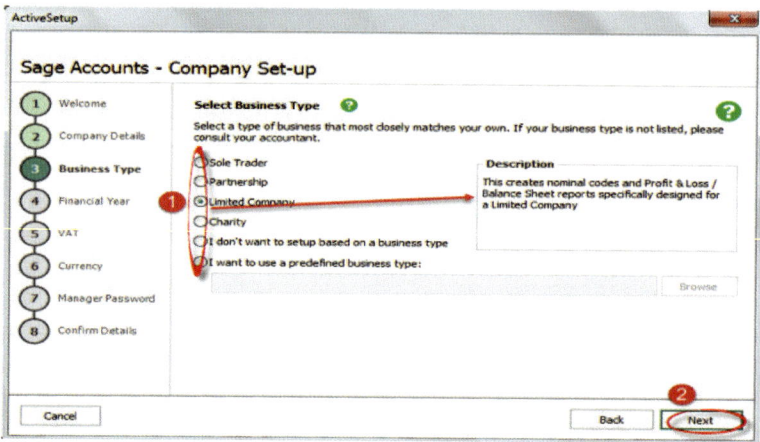

fig. 5

1. Select your business type.

2. Click Next to continue

You will then see a window similar to the one below; asking you to set up the financial year for your business.

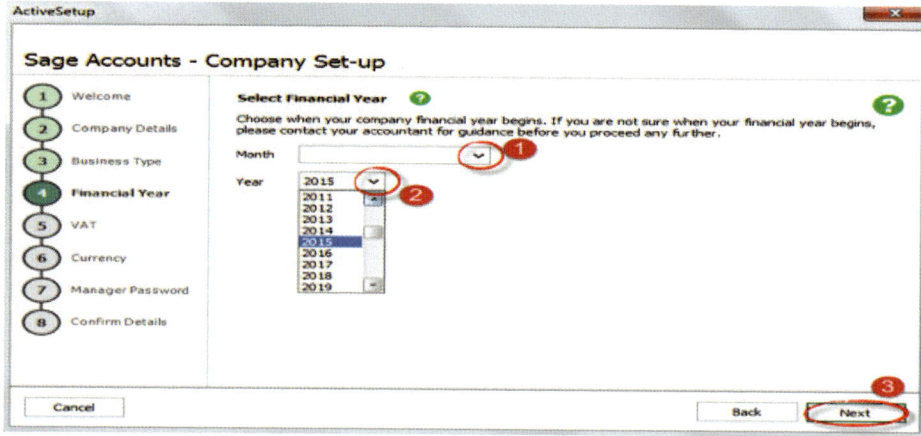

fig. 6

Question for you: What is the difference between a financial year & a tax year?

After you answer the above question, proceed with your company set up.

Now, on the figure above;

1. Click the drop down arrow to select the month the business started trading

2. Click the drop down arrow to select the current financial year of the business

3. Click next to proceed to the next step of set up

You will then see a window similar to the one below – asking you to set up the VAT status of your company on Sage 50.

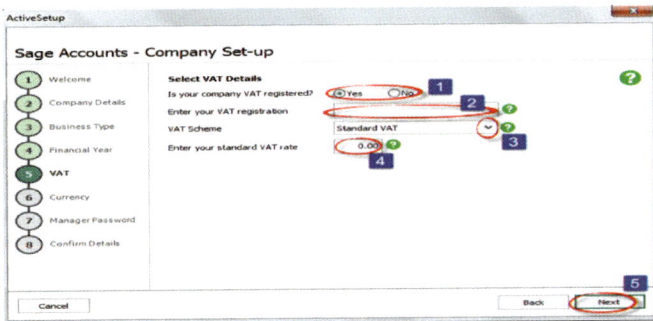

fig. 7

1. Select yes if the business is VAT registered or No if it is not

2. Enter in here the VAT registration number if the business is VAT registered

3. Click the drop down list to select the scheme the business is registered under with HMRC.

4. Type in here the current prevailing rate of VAT depending on the VAT scheme chosen in step 3 above.

5. Click next to continue the set up process

Here is what you will see next as you proceed with the set up; a window requesting you to select the default currency to be used.

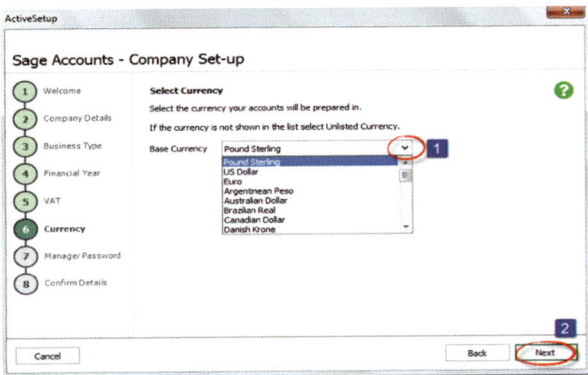

fig. 8

1. Click on the drop down arrow to select the currency the business trades mostly in

2. Click next to continue with the set up process

Next up will be the setup of the password for manager logon.

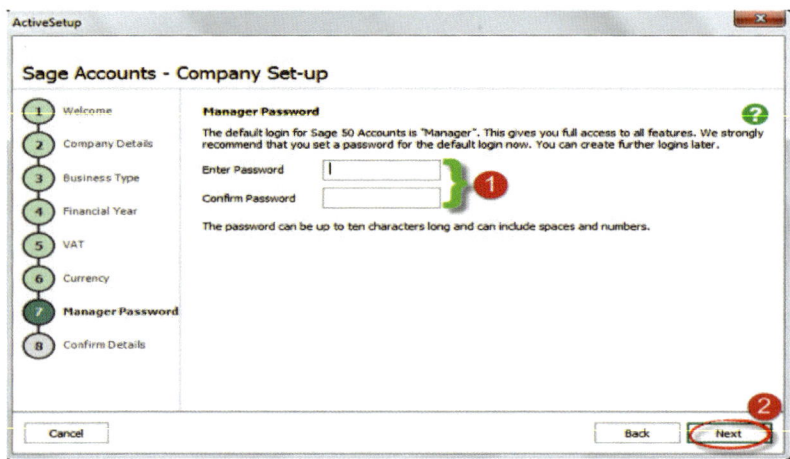

fig. 9

1. Set up and confirm password for the manager login if you wish to

2. Click next to continue to the next step of the set up process

You will then see a window asking you to confirm the details of the new business you have just added to Sage 50. see *Fig. 10* below.

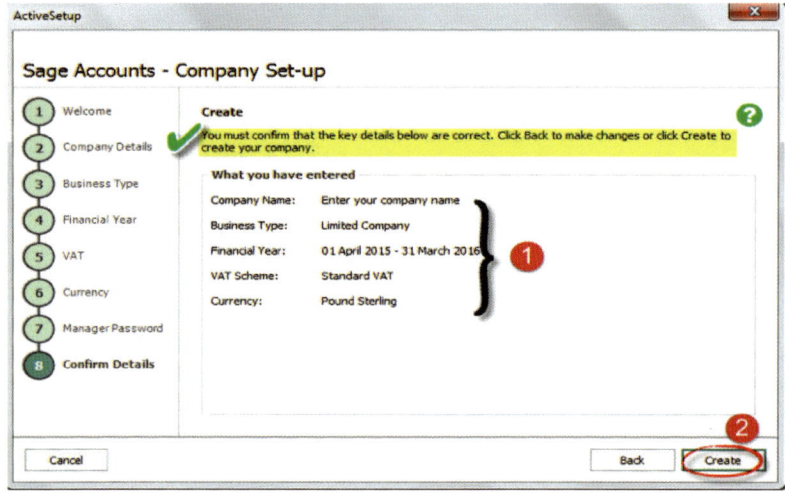

fig. 10

SECTION 1 – GETTING STARTED – SETTING UP

1. *Confirm that the details stated here are meant to be so and then*

2. *Click create to complete the set up of your new company/business in Sage 50 accounts*

Once you click create, you will see the following progress window;

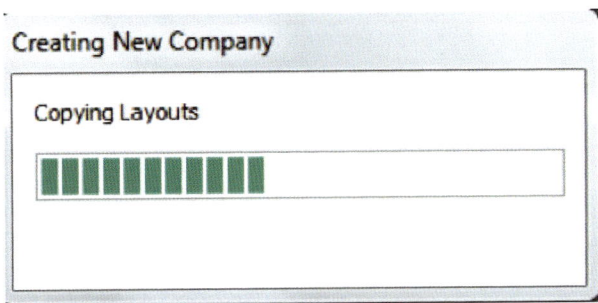

fig. 11

Once the company has been created onto Sage 50, the system will then request you to login – see figure below.

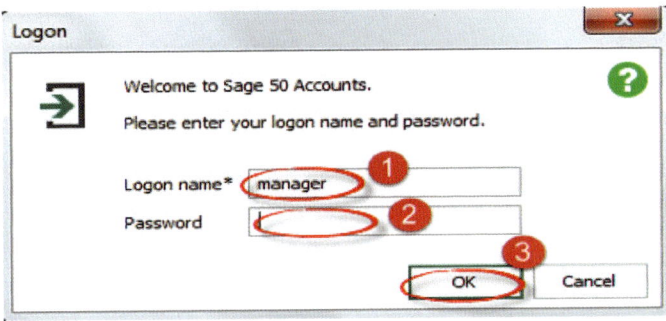

fig. 12

Type in the logon name as manager (this is the default logon name when you first create a new company on Sage 50 accounts).

Enter the password here if you created one during the set up process, if not, just leave it blank.

Click OK to complete logon.

Here is then what you will see next - a window asking whether you want to customise your company or not. Customising your company simply means to be able to setup some defaults so as to save time and reduce potential errors.

THE ACCOUNTS ASSISTANT JOB MANUAL

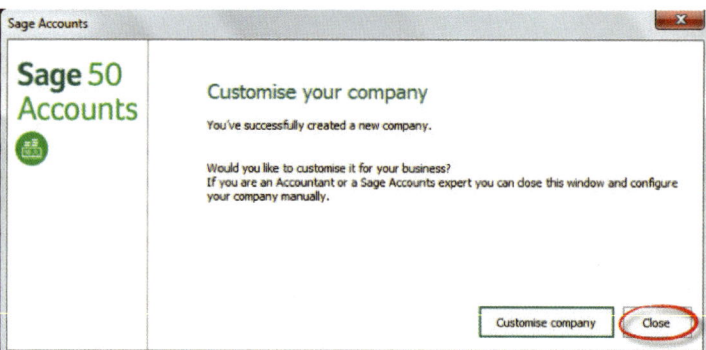

fig. 13

If you so wish to customise your company, then click on customise company otherwise click close.

Once you click close, you will then see your company created on Sage 50 accounts software – see below;

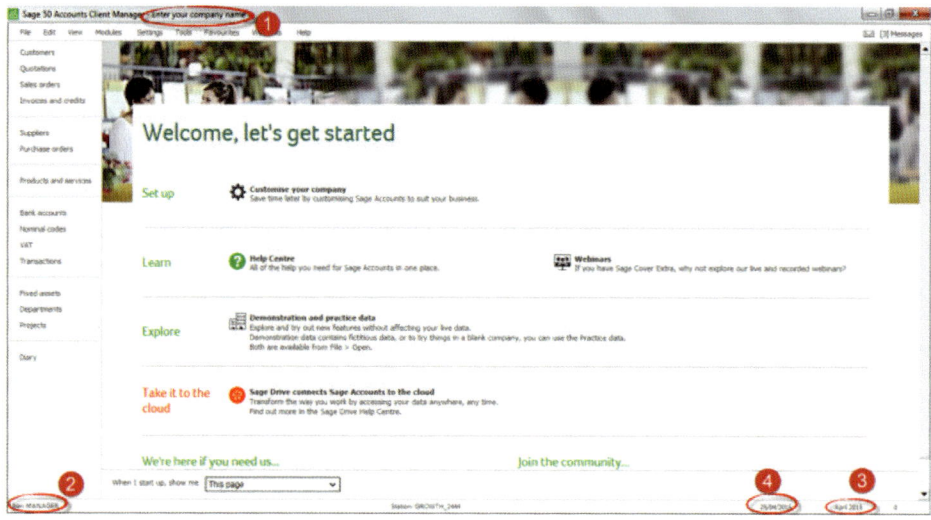

fig. 14

1. This is your company/business name that you created during the set up process

2. This is the user currently logged on to the system

3. This date is the start of the financial year for your business as created during set up

4. This date is picked automatically by the system and it is always by default – todays date. You can however change it to any date within the financial year of the business. See later

If you decide to click customise company instead of close, Sage will basically start up a new window to guide you through setting up defaults for customer & sales, supplier & purchases, banking, products, transactions, services, automatic enrolment.

The customisation set up window looks like this – see below.

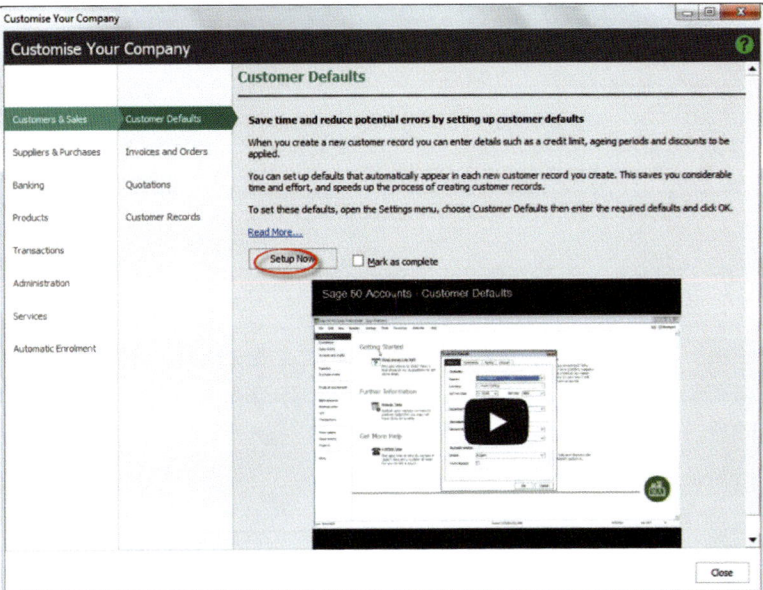

fig. 15

If you so wish to customise your company to save time later and reduce potential errors, then follow through with each of the sections as listed in the figure above. Watch the inset videos and click set up now to set whatever defaults you wish to.

That completes the set up process. Now let's look at the tasks that we need to perform in the accounts assistant role using Sage 50 accounts.

TASK 2

Changing program date & setting login access rights

a. Change program date

This is to ensure that you are doing the postings within the financial year of the business.

Here is what to do:

- *Click on settings then click on change program date from the drop down list that appears. See illustration in the figure below*

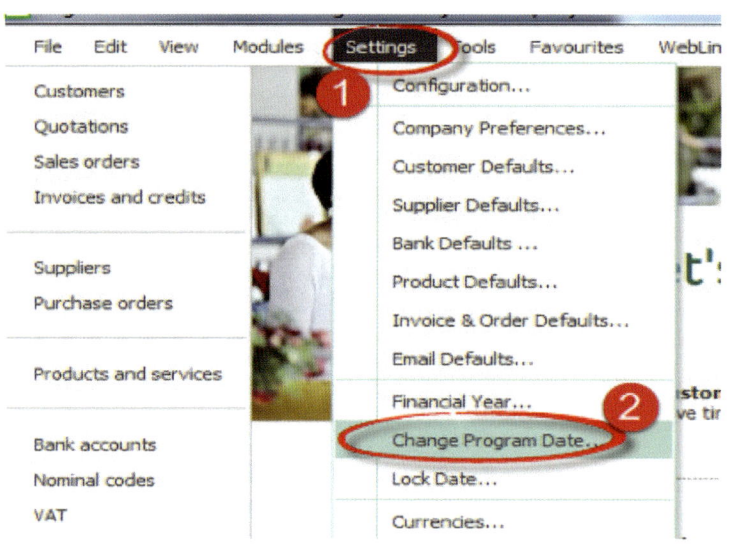

fig. 16

- *When you click on change program date (Step No. 2 in the figure above) the window similar to Fig. 17 in the next page will appear.*

SECTION 1 – GETTING STARTED – SETTING UP

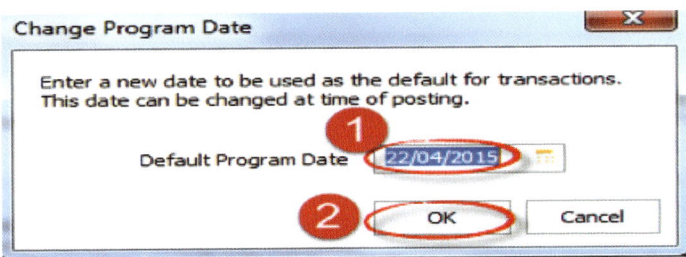

fig. 17

1. Change the default program date to a date within the financial year

2. Click OK to continue. Notice at the bottom left of the Sage software that the program date should change to the one you typed.

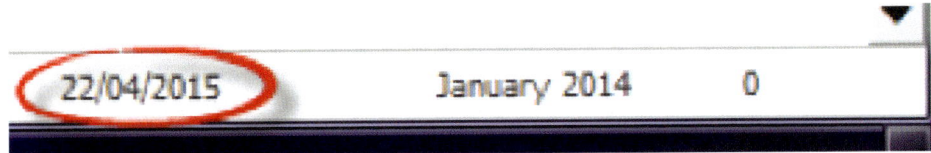

fig. 18

b. Creating your login access rights on Sage 50 Accounts

This is for security of accounting data.

i. Click on settings, then click on access rights - 3rd option from the bottom of the drop down information that appears. See illustration in Fig. 19 in the next page.

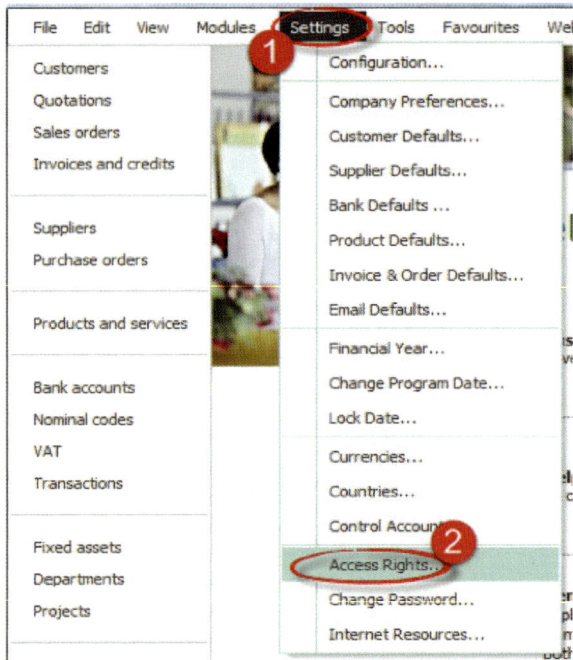

fig. 19

- Once you click access rights – step 2 in the figure above, the user access rights window similar to the one below will appear:

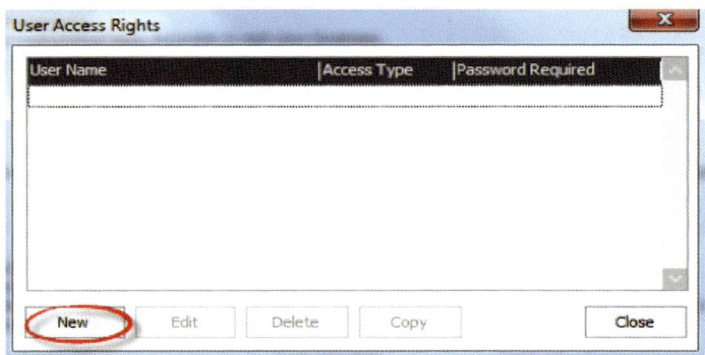

fig. 20

- Click on New and the create new user window similar to Fig. 21 in the next page will appear

SECTION 1 – GETTING STARTED – SETTING UP

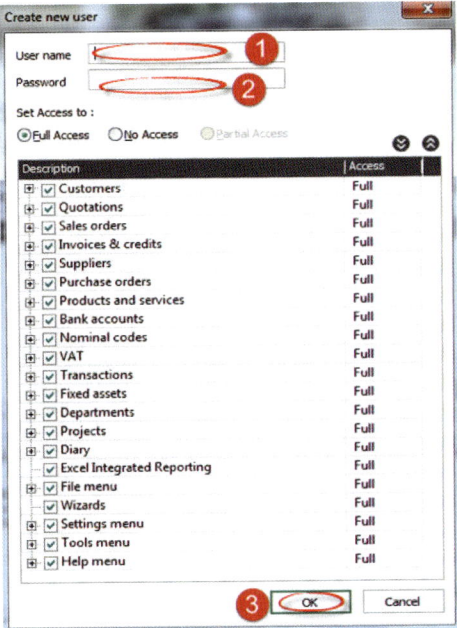

fig. 21

1. Fill up this box with your preferred user name e.g. Trainee.

2. Enter a password here.

3. Click OK to continue.

After you click OK – step 3, a window similar to the one below will appear.

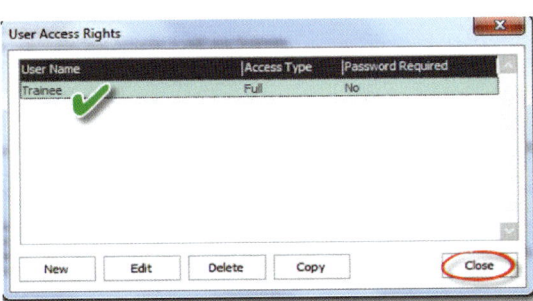

fig. 22

Notice the new user – **Trainee** now shown on the User access rights window.

Click Close to exit the window.

Now log in into the software using the user name you chose. Here is how to do it.

13

THE ACCOUNTS ASSISTANT JOB MANUAL

- Click on File > then click on log off > then type in the username you created > and then click OK (see illustration in the figure below).

fig. 23

Once you click log off, a logon window similar to the one below will appear.

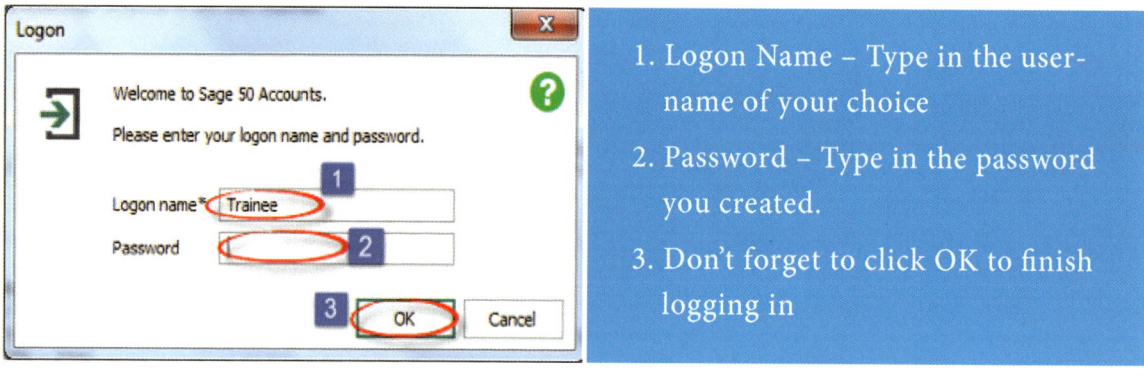

1. Logon Name – Type in the username of your choice
2. Password – Type in the password you created.
3. Don't forget to click OK to finish logging in

fig. 24

Now notice that your login user name is now showing at the bottom left corner of the sage software:

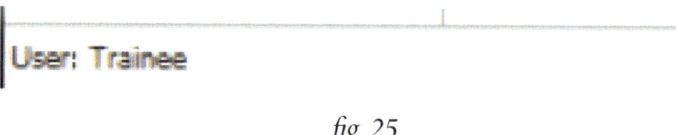

fig. 25

14

SECTION 1 – GETTING STARTED – SETTING UP

TASK 3

Dealing with nominal/Ledger codes and Tax codes

a. Printing out a list of default nominal codes

An account (nominal) code, also called an account code, is used to group accounting information together and enables you to produce summarised accounting reports. The collection of account (nominal) codes makes up the Chart of Accounts.

You can add, edit account (nominal) codes in the chart of accounts. You can create your own customised account (nominal) code structure; every business will have different requirements and Sage 50 accounts allows you this flexibility.

In this book however, we are going to print out the default nominal code list (chart of accounts) that Sage created for us during the company/business set up process earlier on.

Here is what to do:

Follow steps 1 – 3 as shown in the figure below from your Sage 50 accounts software

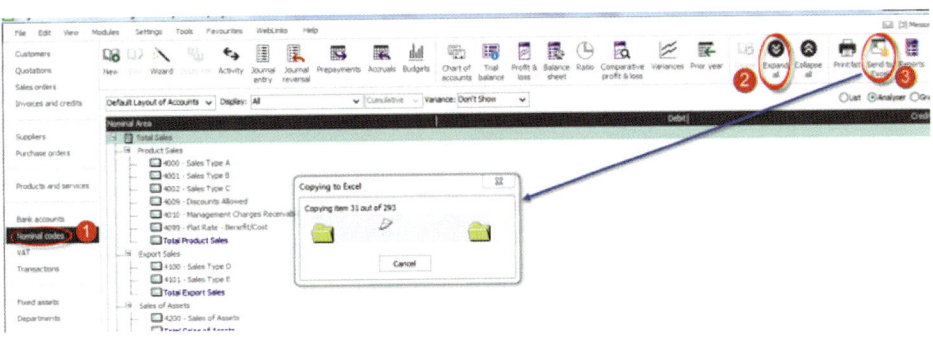

fig. 26

After step 3 in the figure above, the list of nominal codes will be automatically exported to

15

excel and you will notice at the bottom of your computer a highlighted excel document.

fig. 27

Click on that excel document and you will see the excel document with Sage 50 chart of accounts for the business type you selected/chose during set up.

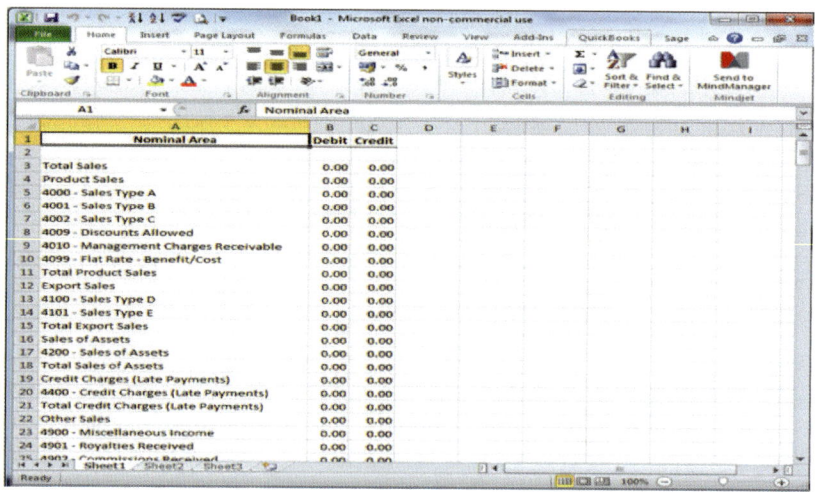

fig. 28

Put borders on the excel document in the figure above and tidy up for easy reference and in the place of the zero's under the debit and credit, mark with an X for the entry each of the nominal codes will have (either debit or credit).

For example Nominal code 4000, will it have a debit or credit balance in the ledger? What about nominal code 0020? And so on and so forth until you exhaust all the nominal codes in the list.

Please note that nominal codes under 4000 are balance sheet codes and those from 4000 and above are profit and loss nominal codes.

b. Printing out a list of tax codes

Tax codes help you keep a track of VAT

Here is what to do to print them out:

- *Click on settings > then click on configurations. See figure below*

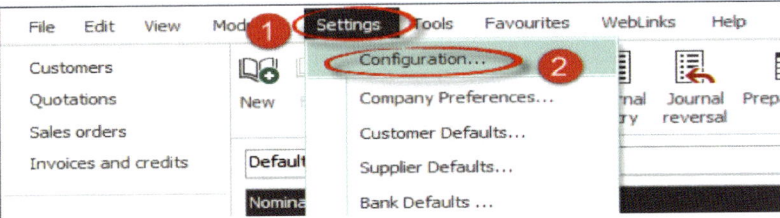

fig. 29

After clicking on configuration (step 2 above) you will notice a window similar to the one below, asking you to confirm whether you want to continue.

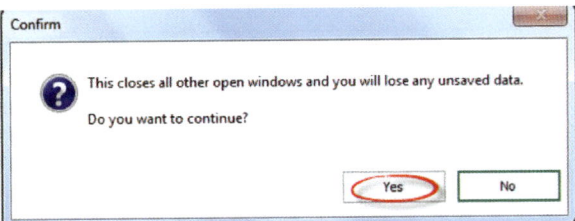

fig. 30

Click yes to continue and you will see a window similar to the one below:

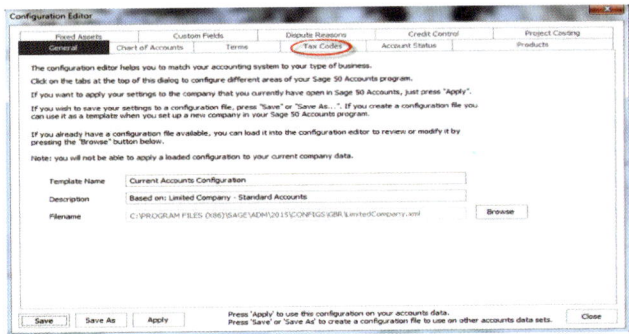

fig. 31

Click on Tax codes.

You will then see a configuration editor window similar to *Fig. 32*

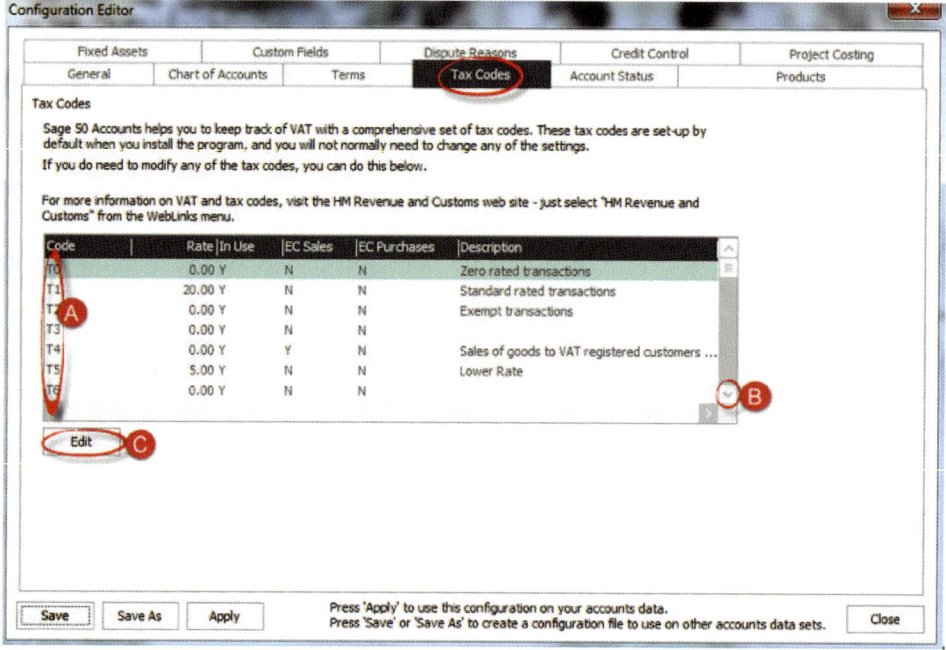

fig. 32

A. This is the list of the tax codes you can use in Sage 50

B. You can click here to scroll down to see a list of all available tax codes in Sage 50

C. Click edit if you want to see the details of any particular tax code in A

The most common tax codes you will use if the business is trading within the UK are T0, T1, T2, T5 and T9. Additionally, if the business is trading with customers and suppliers within the EU, you will also use T8 & T9.

Copy down those common Tax codes.

Remember, if you edit any Tax code, don't forget to click apply.

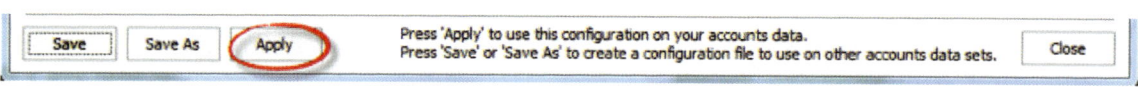

fig. 33

SECTION 1 - GETTING STARTED – SETTING UP

TASK 4
Setting up customer records

To set up a new customer, click on customers > then click on new as illustrated below.

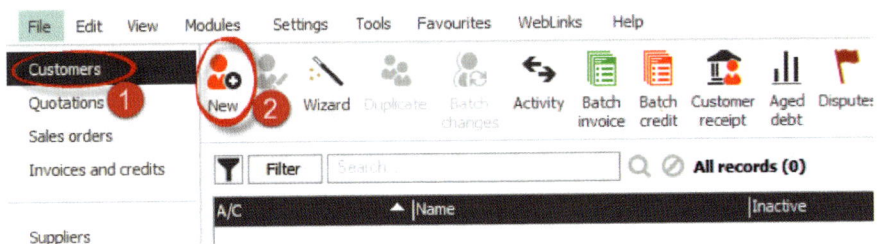

fig. 34

When you click on new (step 2 above) a customer record - setup window similar to the one below will appear.

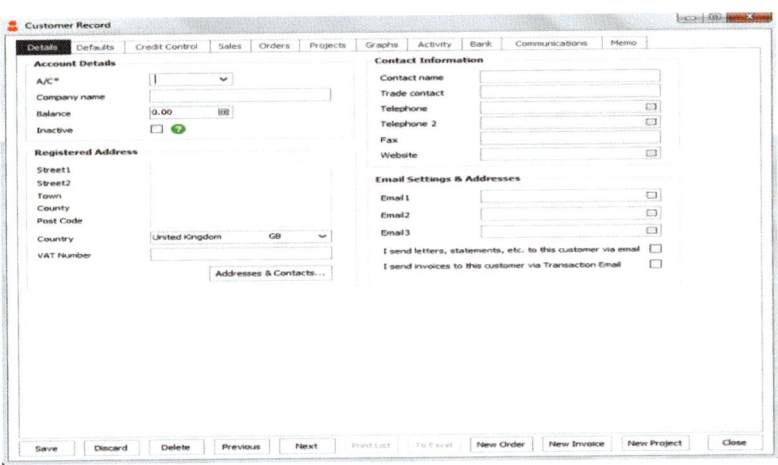

fig. 35

- If you have the customer records at hand, it's now time to fill out the details in the customer records window similar to the one shown above. To do so, we are going to make use of the first 3 tabs on the customer record window – see Fig. 36

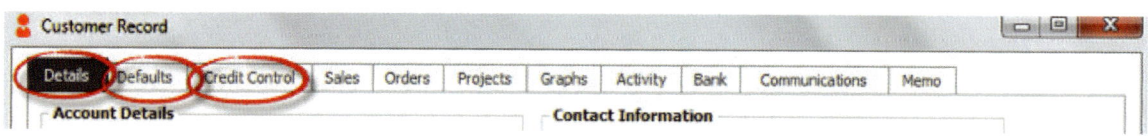

fig. 36

- Select one tab at a time and fill out the details according to the records at hand.

- Let's begin with the details tab, here you will see a box for A/C*. Fill in this box with any reference that will easily help you identify that customer. For example if you have a customer called Blue Ocean Cruisers, you could choose BOC001 as the A/C* reference (the first letters of the words that make up the customer name with 001 added to the end).

- Still on the details tab, if the customer you are creating has a brought forward balance, enter it by clicking on the opening balance window – see below

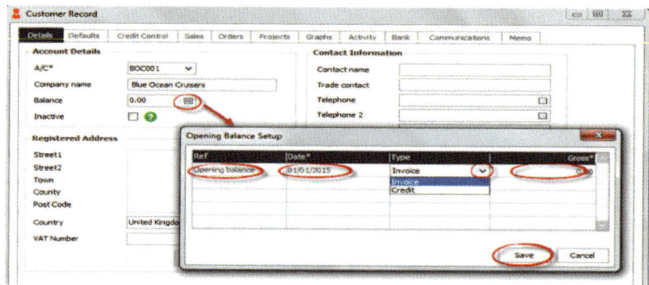

fig. 37

After you have entered the opening balance details (if any) fill out the other defaults tab information such as; address and contact information then the Credit control tab information.

- On the Credit Control tab, fill out all the required information including account setup date and remember to tick terms agreed box at the bottom left of the customer record window and click Save – see below

fig. 38

Once you click save and having entered all the required details, your customer will be created on Sage 50.

SECTION 1 – GETTING STARTED – SETTING UP

TASK 5

Setting up Supplier records

To set up a new supplier, click on supplier > then click on new as illustrated below.

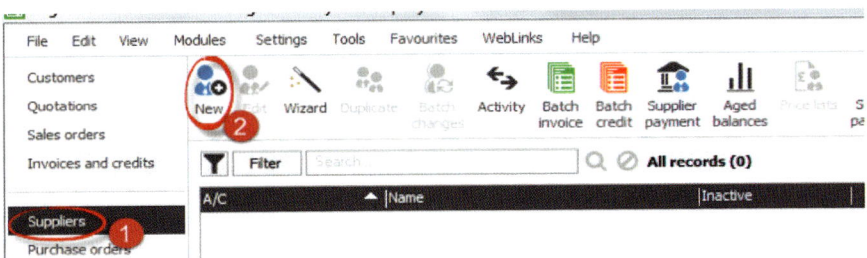

fig. 39

When you click on new (step 2 above) a window similar to the one below will appear.

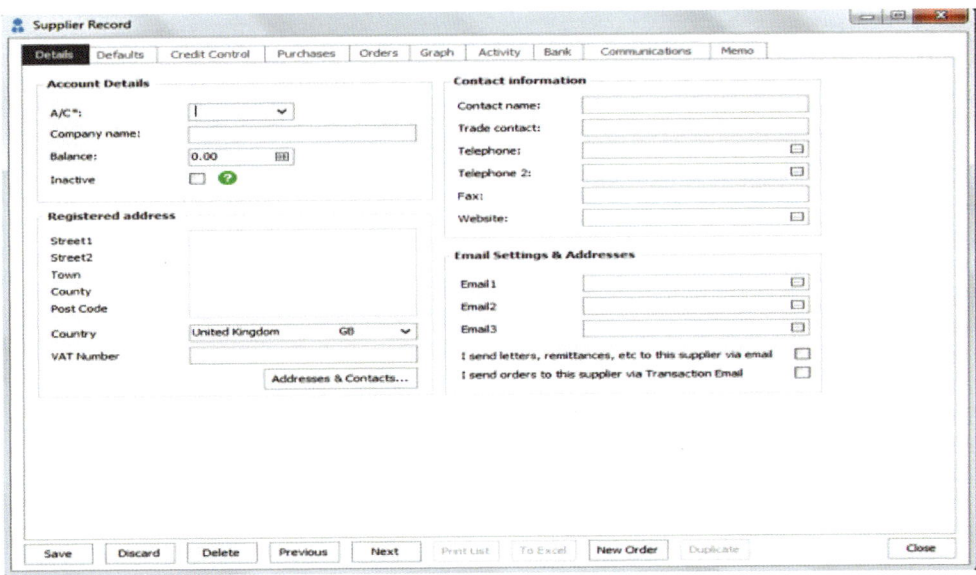

fig. 40

- If you have the supplier records at hand, it's now time to fill out the details in the supplier records window similar to the one shown above. To do that, we are going to make use of the first 3 tabs on the supplier record window – see Fig 41.

21

THE ACCOUNTS ASSISTANT JOB MANUAL

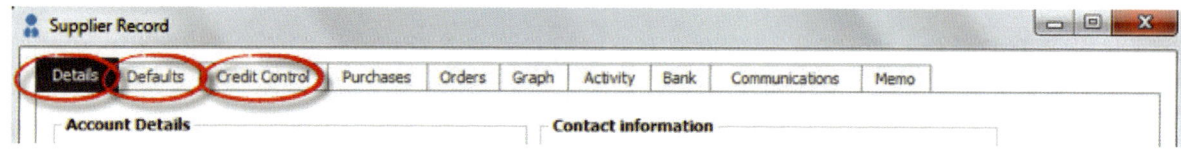

fig. 41

- Select one tab at a time and fill out the details according to the records at hand.

- On the Details tab, you will see a box for A/C*. Fill in this box with any reference that will easily help you identify that supplier. For example if you have a supplier called Bilabong, you could choose BILA001 as the A/C* reference (the first letters of the words that make up the supplier name with 001 added to the end. That's it, that simple

- Still on the details tab, if you owe the supplier you are creating some money enter it as opening balance by clicking on the opening balance window – see below

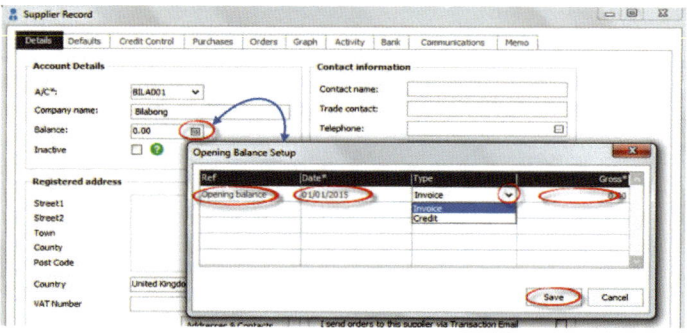

fig. 42

After you have entered the opening balance details (if any) fill out the other defaults tab information like the registered address & contact information then click on the Credit control tab.

- On the Credit Control tab and fill out the necessary details and remember to tick terms agreed box at the bottom left of the supplier record window and click Save – see Fig. 43.

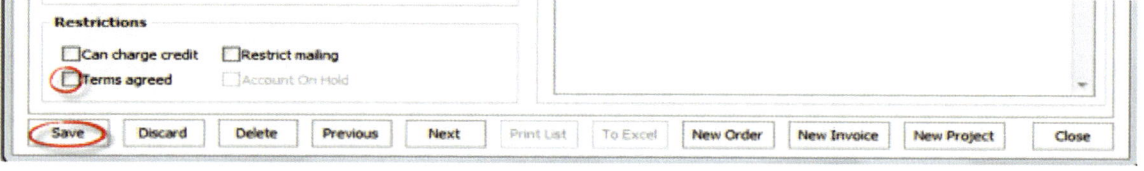

fig. 43

Once you click save and having entered all the required details, your supplier will be created on Sage 50.

SECTION 1 – GETTING STARTED – SETTING UP

TASK 6

Setting up product/service details

Product records can store lots of useful information about your products and services, like the amount you have in stock, and integrate with other features like invoicing to help streamline your data entry later on.

Within a product record, there are various tabs to record information. Most of the critical information is held in the Details tab.

To create a new product/service record, click on products and services > then click on new as illustrated below.

fig. 44

When you click on new (step 2 above) a window similar to the one in *Fig. 45* will appear.

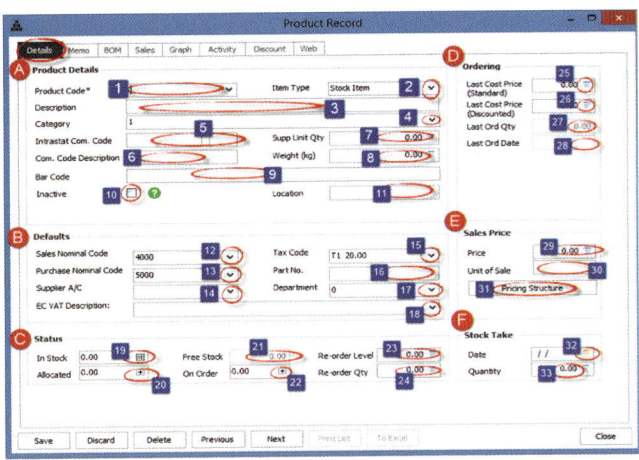

fig. 45

23

Here are the details of how to fill out the information required in the details tab of the product record.

A. Product details.

1. You can enter up to 30 characters for the product code. You can use A-Z, 0-9, /.-# but not spaces or commas. Each different product must have its own unique code. Please note that: Once you create a stock code you cannot change it. If you want to change the code you need to create a new product record.

2. From the drop-down list, choose the type of product record. The product record can be a Stock Item, Service Item or Non-Stock Item.

Service Item is only available in Sage 50 Accounts Professional. See *Fig. 46*.

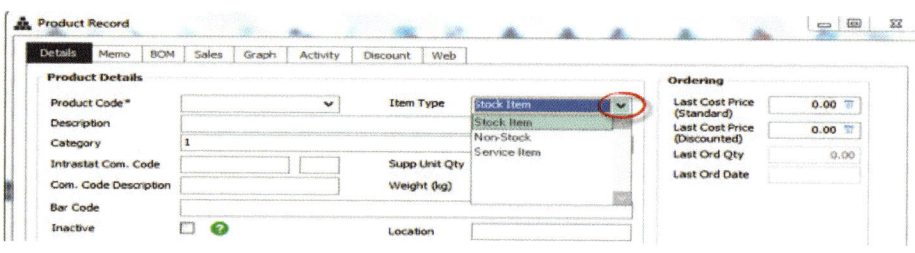

fig. 46

3. Enter the product name or description, up to 60 characters.

4. From the drop-down list you can choose one of the 999 category codes available for reporting purposes. See figure below.

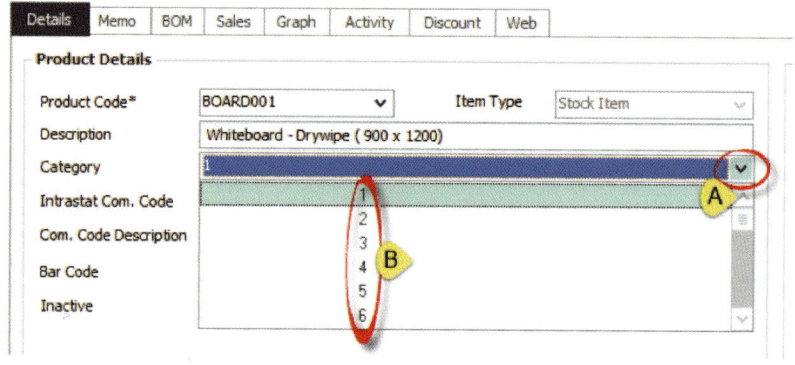

fig. 47

You can set the category codes B in the figure above by clicking settings, then Configuration then Products.

5. *Enter here the item's commodity code. For HMRC or Revenue to accept your Intrastat returns this must be eight numeric characters.*

    The last two digits are for TARIC purposes when dealing with import duty and can be used in customised reports to show the full 10 digits.

    For further information about commodity codes, please contact your relevant tax authority. A UK business should refer to HMRC www.hmrc.gov.uk A business in the Republic of Ireland should refer to the Revenue Commissioners www.revenue.ie

6. *If required, enter a description for your commodity code here.*

7. *Enter here any supplementary units. For each Commodity Code, you must report either the net mass, or both the net mass and the supplementary unit quantities.*

8. *Enter in here the weight of your product in kilograms. You must record this if you produce Intrastat Supplementary Declaration information.*

9. *Enter a series of alphanumeric characters, up to 60 characters in length. You can then add these bar codes on to your product layouts.*

10. *To prevent any further activity on the record, and if required, exclude this product from the Products and services window and selection lists, select this check box.*

11. *Enter in here the location of the product item, using up to 16 characters.*

B. Defaults

12. *Choose the sales nominal code you want associated with the item when you create an invoice or order.*

    You can override this if you select the Use Default Nominal Code for Sales check box from within the Customer record > Defaults tab.

13. *Choose the purchases nominal code you want to use when you create a purchase order for this item. You can override this if you select the Use Default Nominal Code for Purchases check box from within the Supplier Record > Defaults tab.*

    Please note that this option is only available in Accounts Professional version of Sage 50

14. Enter the account code for the supplier of this product.

15. Choose the default VAT rate to apply, when you create a product invoice or credit note and when you create a sales or purchase order for this product.

    You can change this tax code when you enter invoices or orders, if required.

16. You can enter a product reference number here, up to 16 characters, for example a suppliers reference or part number.

17. Choose a department between 0 and 999. You can set up the departments by clicking on Department > **Select Reference** > **edit**.

18. Click the drop down menu to choose an EC Sales description.

    Three default descriptions are provided, and you can create a further four additional messages. If required, you can amend the descriptions within Settings then click on Company Preferences then selecting VAT then click on EC VAT Descriptions.

C.   Status

19. This is the quantity of this product currently in stock.

    This figure increases when you record an adjustment in for this product, when you record a purchase order delivery of this product or when you post a credit note for this product using the Product Credit Note option from the Invoicing window.

    This figure decreases when you record an adjustment out for this product, when you despatch a sales order which includes this product or when you post an invoice for this product using the Product Invoice option from the Invoicing window.

    You can also increase or decrease the stock level using the Product Transfer option.

Click the small OB option in box 19 to enter the opening balance quantity for the product if there is an opening balance for this product. See figure below.

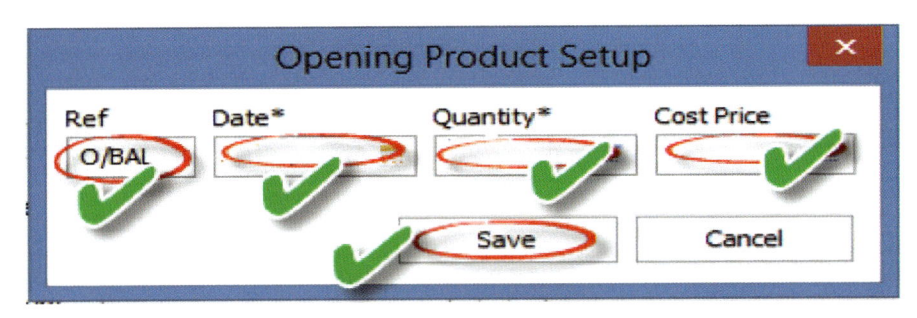

fig. 48

Ref - Enter a reference for the opening balance. By default this is O/BAL.

Date* - Enter the date of the opening balance.

Quantity* - Enter the quantity in stock for the opening balance.

Cost Price - Enter the cost price for the stock. This value is used to calculate the values on your stock valuation reports.

Don't forget to click Save.

20. This is the quantity of the product that has been part or fully allocated on sales orders and projects, but has not yet been despatched. To see the orders the stock is allocated to, click the plus . Please note that the allocated box is only available in Sage 50 Accounts Professional only

21. Free stock - this is the In stock total minus the Allocated stock total.

    This appears in any window where you choose the product code.

22. On order – this option is available only in the Sage 50 accounts professional version only. This is basically the quantity of the product that is on order through your purchase orders.

    To see which orders that have the stock on order, click the plus .

23. This option is only available on Sage 50 Accounts Plus and Accounts Professional only

    Enter here the quantity of stock that you would normally re-order. The quantity you enter here appears automatically for you, when you raise a purchase order or use the Shortfall option for this product, but you can overwrite it.

24. Enter in here the quantity of stock at which new stock should be ordered.

    If the stock level falls below this value, the item appears in red in the Products window and appears on the Re-order Levels and Shortfall reports. If you leave this as 0.00 it doesn't appear on the reports.

This option is yet again available only in Sage 50 Accounts Plus and Accounts Professional only.

D. Ordering

25. This is the latest cost price for the product item. It is taken from the last entry that has been made using either the Opening Balance option, the Adjustments In option, Purchase Order Processing, or the Global Changes option. No discount is taken into account.

26. This is the discounted cost price for the product item. It is taken from the last entry that has been made using either the Opening Balance option, the Adjustments In option, Purchase Order Processing, or the Global Changes option

27. This shows the quantity of this product ordered from the last purchase order raised, after it has been put on order. This option is only in Accounts Professional version of Sage 50

28. This shows the date of the last purchase order raised for this product, after it has been put on order. This appears only in Sage 50 Accounts Professional only.

E. Sales Price

29. Enter here the net selling price of the product, excluding VAT, which is used for sales orders, product invoices and credit notes.

30. Here you can write things like each, box, and 10 pack to describe the unit of sale. You can use up to 8 characters. This is used for reference only and is not used in any calculation of prices.

31. This option is only available in Sage 50 Accounts Plus and Accounts Professional.

If you need to create a special price for this product, click Pricing Structure then complete, as required.

F. Stock Take

32. Enter the date of your last stock take here. This date is for reference purposes only.

33. If you previously did a stock take, enter the stock quantity of this product at your last stock take here. This quantity is used for information only and does not affect your In Stock quantity.

TASK 7

Setting up opening balances for ledger accounts

Example: 1 – Using nominal codes

Here are 3 ledger accounts with opening balances:

- Goods for resale > debit of £5,000

- Motor vehicle > debit of £15,000

- VAT on Sales > credit balance of £2,378

Let's enter the last one – VAT on sales for illustration purposes.

Here is what to do – see the steps in the figure below;

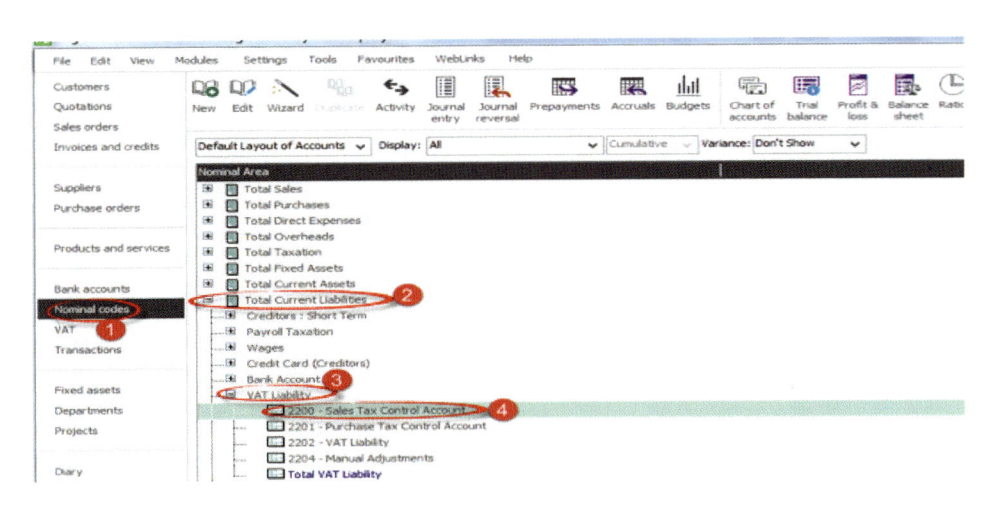

fig. 49

When following the steps above, double click at step 2 & 3 or click on the + sign to expand and see available sub items.

At step 4, just double click on the selected item and a window similar to the one below will appear. Follow the inset steps to complete the opening balance record.

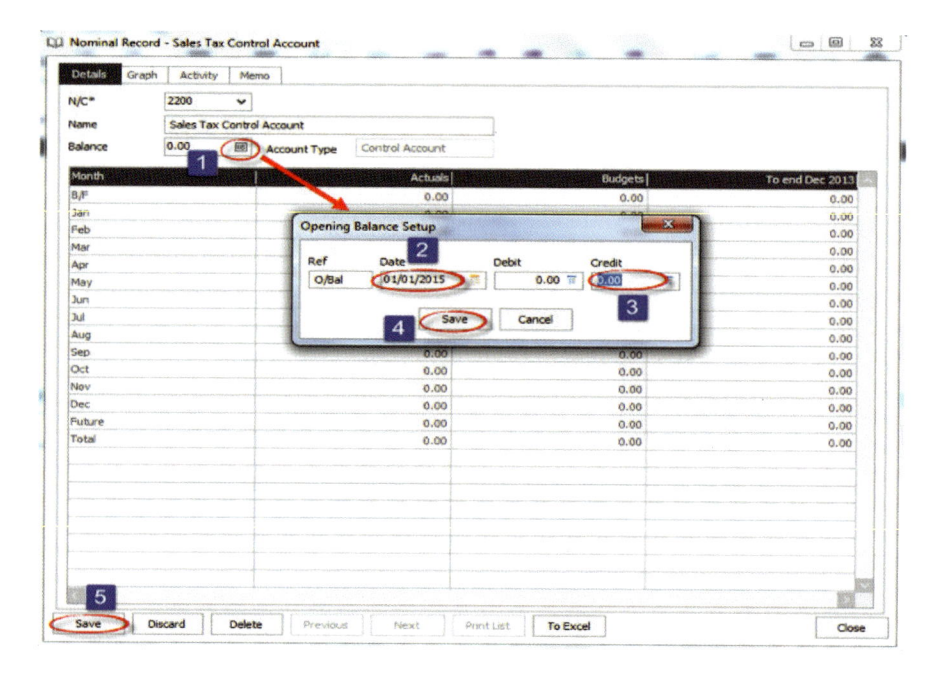

fig. 50

That's the procedure to follow when entering opening balances.

Now you try it by entering the other two remaining opening balances in this example, i.e. the goods for resale and the motor vehicles opening balances.

As you will most often be using a closing trial balance or closing balance sheet as the source for the opening balances, print out the report of either the trial balance or balance sheet (whichever you used) after you have entered all the opening balances from it and compare it to the original document you used (original balance sheet or trial balance).

The point here is that, both your original trial balance or balance sheet and the new one you print after entering the opening balances should exactly be the same and that is your evidence that you have correctly entered all the opening balances.

Example 2: setting up opening balances using opening balances wizard in Sage.

Click on Tools and then select opening balances from the drop down menu that appears as shown below.

fig. 51

Once you click on opening balances as illustrated in the figure above, the figure similar to the one in *Fig. 52* will appear:

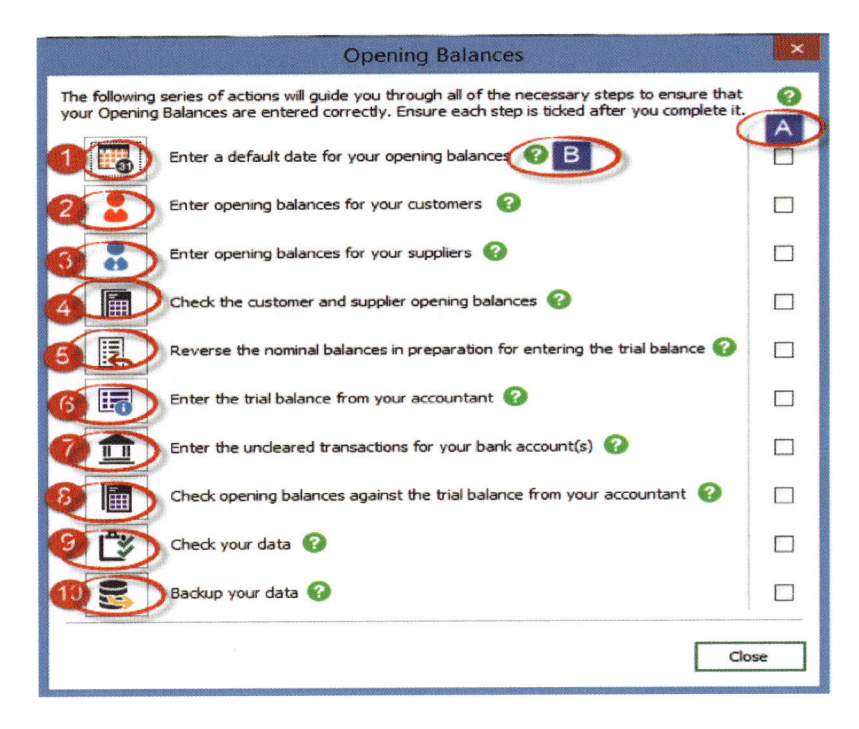

fig. 52

- *To enter the opening balances follow the steps 1- 10 as illustrated in the figure above*
- *Click on each of the cycled items from 1-10 in sequence. If you are not sure what to do at each step, click on the green question mark – illustrated by letter B.*
- *Once you have completed each step, remember to tick it as done from the tick boxes illustrated under letter A in the figure above*

You will be given a list of opening balances for customers, suppliers, and a copy of the closing trial balance from the prior period/year and you will be expected to use it to set up opening balances in Sage 50 as illustrated above.

> **"Tell me, and I will forget. Show me, and I may remember. Involve me and I will understand"**
>
> *–Confucius (551-479)*

SECTION 2
PURCHASE LEDGER

TASK 8

Creating a purchase order in Sage 50 Professional

a. Order details

This option is only available in Sage 50 Accounts Professional only.

The Purchase orders module can be used to keep track of the products that you buy. You can create and print orders to send to your suppliers. The Purchase orders option is directly linked to your product records, so the orders you produce automatically update your records with the order details.

To start creating a purchase order, click on Purchase orders > New. See figure below.

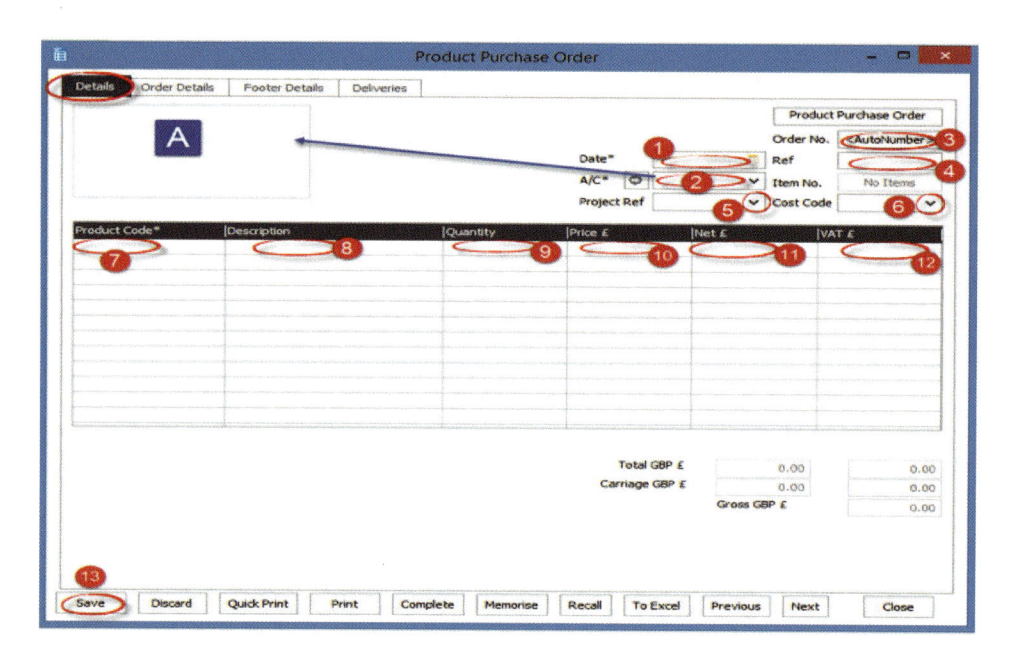

fig. 53

Enter the purchase order details as follows.

1. *Type in here your date as required. Note that the current software date appears by default when this window first appears.*

2. *Select from the drop-down list the supplier account reference and enter it here. The supplier's name and address appears in box A.*

   If you enter an account code that is not already set up, the drop-down list appears. You can then either select another account or create a new one by clicking New.

   A warning appears if the supplier account you select is on hold or if terms haven't been agreed.

3. *When you create a new purchase order, <AutoNumber> appears in this box. Purchase order numbers are not assigned until the order has been saved.*

   Each time you create and save a new purchase order, the order number is increased by one. If you want to start numbering your orders at a particular number, you must change the numbering sequence in Settings > Invoice & Order Defaults > Options.

   If you want to edit an existing purchase order, enter the order number of the order that you want to edit.

4. *Use the Ref box to enter your own reference for the purchase order. You can use up to seven characters*

5. *This box appears if project costing is switched on. If the order is for a project, you can enter the project reference here to link the order with the project.*

   You can use the drop-down list to search for and select the required project record.

   Please note that to successfully create the order, the project status must enable postings.

6. *This box appears if project costing is switched on. If the order is for a project, enter the cost code to be used to apply the value of the goods.*

   You can use the drop-down list to search for and select the required cost code. If you enter an unknown cost code you are given the list of existing cost codes to select from.

7. *Enter a product code that you've previously created in the Products module or use the drop-down list to locate the required product.*

   In addition to the normal product codes you can also enter special non-product codes, where:

   - *S1 = Special product item with price and VAT amount.*
   - *S2 = Special product item that is exempt for VAT.*
   - *S3 = Special service item with price and VAT amount.*
   - *M = Message line. Add any text in the main body of the purchase order.*

If special product codes don't appear in the product code list, open Settings > Invoice & Order Defaults > select the Show special product codes in Invoicing / SOP / POP check box.

Please note that: You can't change the product code on a purchase order if the order shows as on-order or you've received quantity for that product.

If you open an existing order that contains products with on-order or received quantities, the product code is not enabled, and you can't change it.

To change the product code on an order if it has an on-order quantity, you must first reverse the on-order status using the Amend deliveries option.

If a product shows a received quantity, you must reverse the delivery manually, taking the supplier and stock into account where appropriate, and re-enter an order as you require.

8. *The description of your product from the product record appears here.*

   You can change this if required. Double-click in this box or click the box > press F3.

9. *Enter the quantity of stock you want to order. The Re-Order Quantity from the product record, appears automatically, but you can change this if necessary.*

10. *The unit price from the product record appears here. If a special product code has been entered, the value entered in the Edit Item Line window appears here. You can amend this.*

11. *The net value calculates automatically and can't be edited.*

12. *The VAT amount appears here and can't be edited.*

13. *Don't forget to click Save to save the order details.*

SECTION 2 - PURCHASE LEDGER

b. Placing the order

After you create a purchase order you must put it on order before you can record any deliveries for it. This updates the on order levels for each of the appropriate product records. To save time, use the Place orders option to automatically put a batch of purchase orders on order. See illustration in figure below.

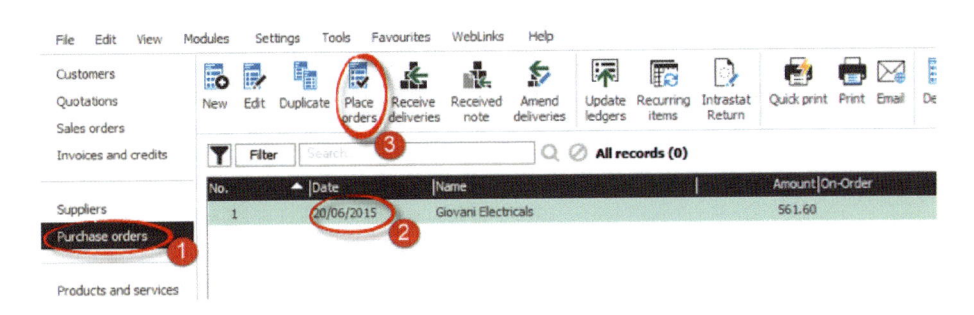

fig. 541. Click on purchase orders,

2. *Then highlight all the purchase orders you want* to *place orders on*

3. *Click place orders and a window with a message similar to the one in the figure below will appear*

fig. 55

You can choose order now or order later. For the purpose of our illustration, choose order later by clicking on it.

c. Receiving deliveries or purchase order(s)

The Receive deliveries option saves you time by automatically updating your stock and creating a purchase invoice. Once the status of the order is on order there are different ways to record its delivery, depending on what you want to achieve. See figure below.

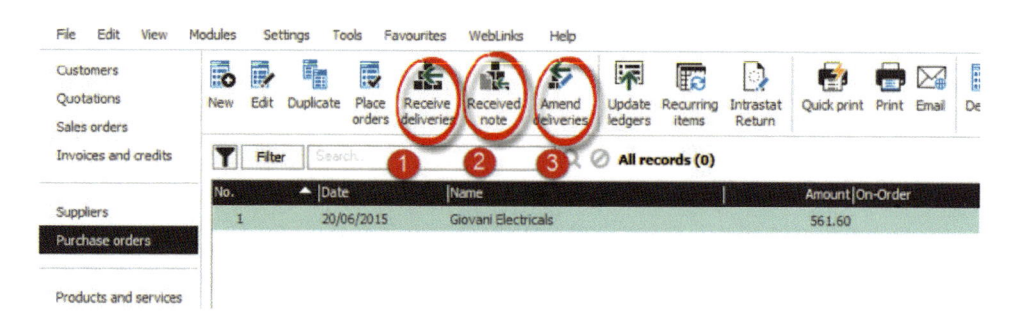

fig. 56

You can use the:

1. Receive deliveries

This option posts a goods in adjustment (GI) and the order status changes to COMPLETE.

2. Received notes

You can record delivery of all or part of the order using this option.

As with Receive deliveries and Amend deliveries, this option updates the product records and generates a GI – Goods In adjustment.

Use this option when you need to generate multiple goods received notes. Each delivery generates a goods received note.

3. Amend deliveries

Using this option increases the stock levels, generates a GI, for the quantity that is delivered by the supplier.

If all of the stock isn't delivered, this option marks the purchase order as PART. When all stock is delivered, the order is marked as COMPLETE.

SECTION 2 - PURCHASE LEDGER

For the purpose of our illustration, we are going to use option 1 – Receive deliveries.

Now, click on receive deliveries window.

The following message will appear. See figure below.

fig. 57

Click yes to continue.

Once you click yes as illustrated in the figure above, a window similar to *Fig. 58* will appear.

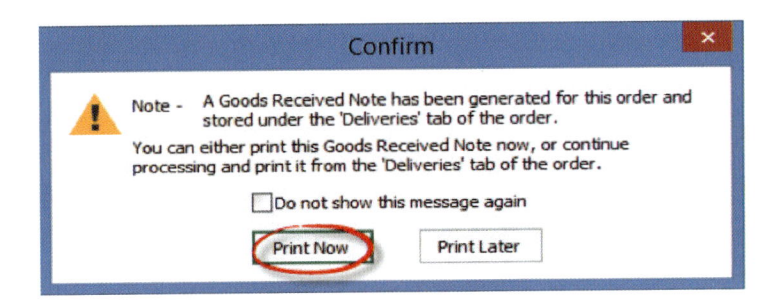

fig. 58

Click print now and a print window similar to the figure below will appear.

fig. 59

TASK 9

Processing supplier invoices and credit notes.

Creating purchase invoices from your purchase orders

You can use the Update ledgers option to create purchase invoices directly from your purchase orders. This saves time, as you don't have to manually enter details of the orders to create an invoice.

If you create an invoice from a purchase order, Y appears in the Posted column.

The figure below shows how you can create a purchase invoice from purchase orders.

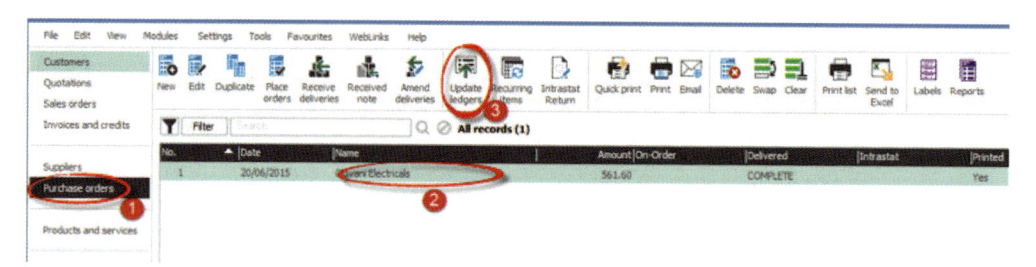

fig. 601. Click on purchase orders

2. Click to highlight the completed orders you want to create invoices from

3. Click update ledgers *and a window similar to the one below will appear*

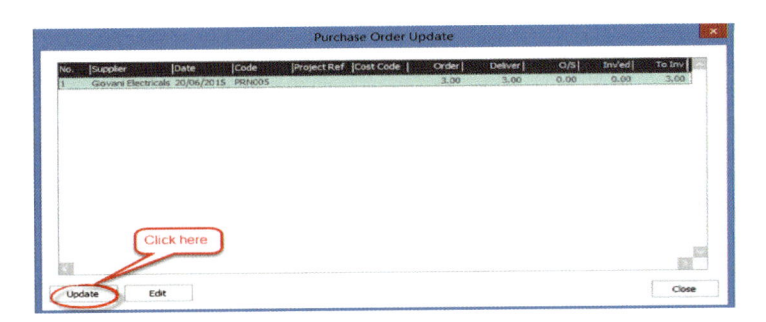

fig. 61

Click update to continue.

A window similar the figure below will appear once you click on update as illustrated above.

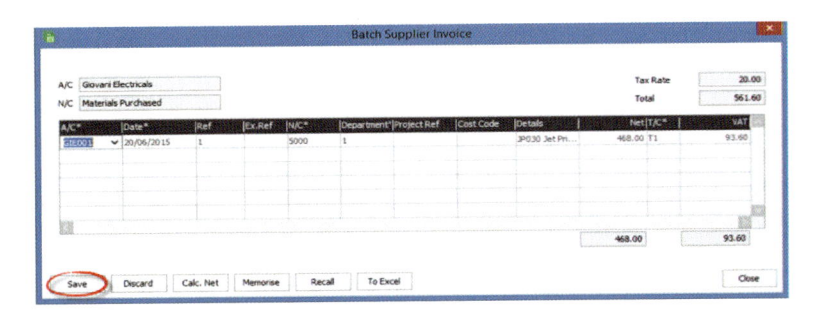

fig. 62

Check to confirm that the details of the entries are correct then click Save.

Purchase invoice entry via batch invoice

i. Add together the amounts in list of purchase invoices to be entered into Sage

ii. Enter the purchase invoices onto Sage 50 accounts by selecting suppliers then clicking **Batch invoice**

iii. Using the invoices enter the details of each invoice on the window that appears as shown below:

iv. Enter a pencil tick by the gross amount of the invoice when entered.

v. The total of all the invoices entered (the Batch Total on the Sage screen) should equal the add-list produced in step iv above.

vi. Once the totals agree, click save to post in to the ledgers.

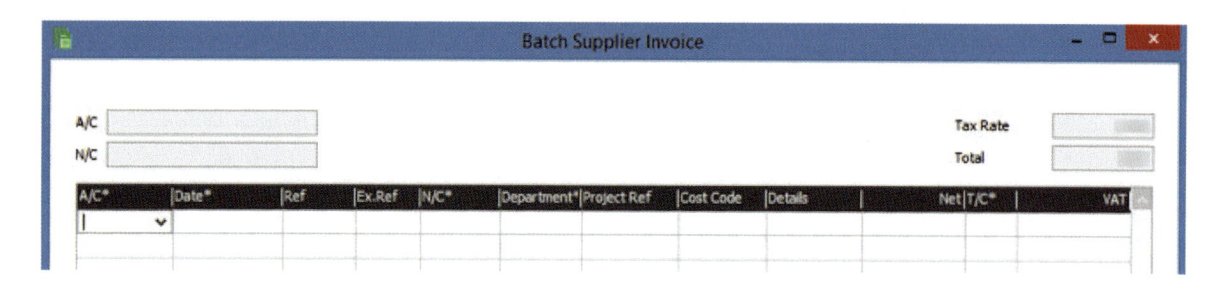

fig. 63

A/C –	the purchase ledger/supplier account reference
Date –	the date on the invoice
Ref -	the invoice number
Ex Ref –	leave blank or hide it by right clicking on the black area & unticking Ex Ref from the drop down list that appears
N/C –	the nominal code for that type of purchase (e.g. 5000 for goods for resale, 7201 for gas)
Dept –	the department reference number (if applicable, otherwise right click on it and untick it to remove it from the visible dialogue box)
Project Ref –	the project reference number (if applicable, otherwise right click on it and un tick it to remove it from the visible dialogue box)
Details –	a unique entry number which is usually your filing reference number followed by any description you would find useful
Net –	the net amount of the purchase per the invoice
T/C –	the VAT rate used (e.g. T1 for standard rated)
VAT –	this should be calculated automatically by Sage but must agree to the VAT shown on the invoice

Don't forget to click Save.

Purchase credit note entry

The fastest way to enter a purchase credit note on to sage 50 accounts; click on suppliers >then click on batch credit – see below.

SECTION 2 - PURCHASE LEDGER

fig. 64

After clicking batch credit as illustrated above, fill out the window that appears as shown below; first make an add list of the total value of all the credit notes to be entered into Sage 50 accounts.

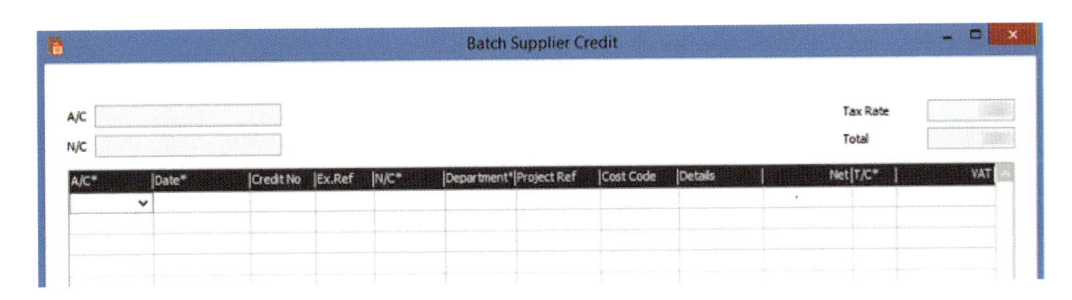

fig. 65

Enter the details of each credit note as follows.

A/C – the purchase ledger/supplier account reference

Date – the date on the invoice

Credit Ref – the credit note number

Ex Ref – leave blank or hide it by right clicking on the black area & unticking Ex Ref from the drop down list that appears

N/C – the nominal code for that type of original purchase (e.g. 5000 for goods for resale, 7201 for gas)

Dept – the department reference number (if applicable, otherwise right click on it and untick it to remove it from the visible dialogue box)

Project Ref – the project reference number (if applicable, otherwise right click on it and un tick it to remove it from the visible dialogue box)

Details – a unique entry number which is usually your filing reference number

43

                  followed by any description you would find useful

Net –   the net amount of the purchase per the invoice

T/C –   the VAT rate used (e.g. T1 for standard rated)

VAT –   this should be calculated automatically by Sage but must agree to the VAT shown on the invoice

Don't forget to click save after you have entered the details.

TASK 10

Paying suppliers

Please note: before making payments to suppliers, it is advisable that a bank reconciliation should always be done.

a. Doing payment runs

Click on bank accounts then click on batch supplier payment, select how much you want to pay each supplier (under instruction form finance manager) out of the outstanding values.

Make a list of all suggested payments, print it out, attach relevant invoices and take it to the manager for authorisation. See below.

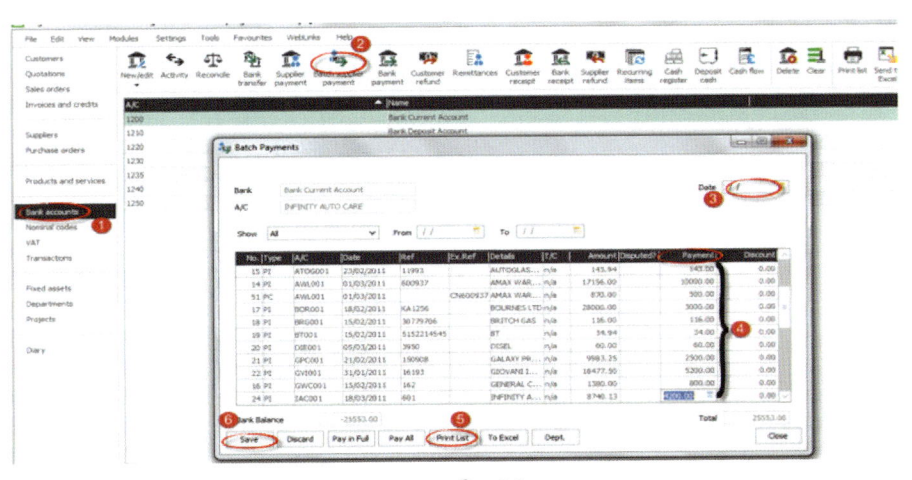

fig. 66

Steps: (from 4, do 1-3 first)

    4. Suggest payment amounts

    5. Print the list and take to the manager with supplier invoices attached

    6. Don't forget to come back and click Save once the list is approved, otherwise make necessary amendments and adjustments before clicking save because once you click save, the suggested payments will be posted in the ledgers as payments to suppliers you suggested payments to.

b.   Paying suppliers via supplier payment

Enter the payment by clicking on Bank accounts, then highlight Bank Current account (1200), then Click on Supplier payment.

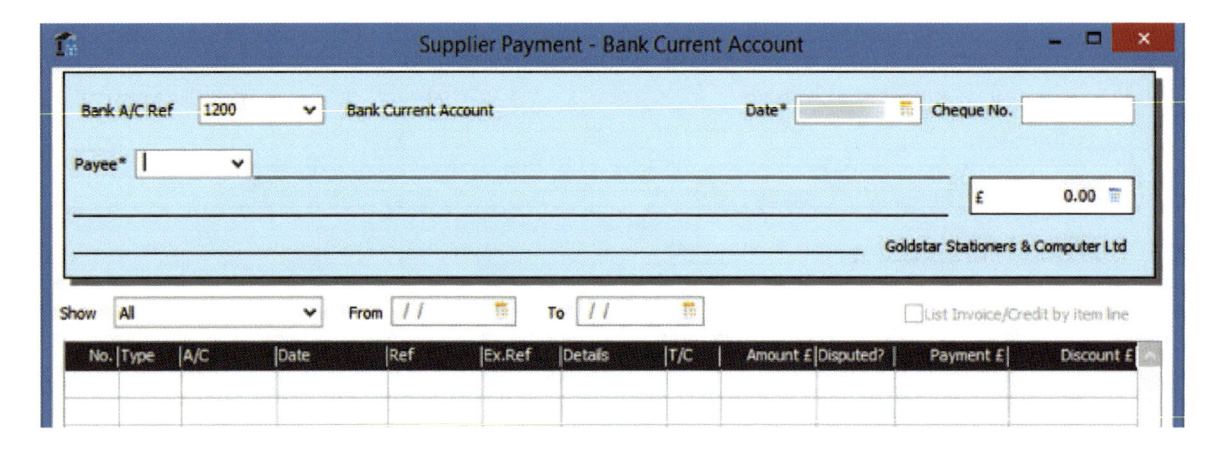

fig. 67

For each payment enter:

Payee –   the purchase ledger/supplier account reference code

The supplier Name should come up automatically- but do check that it is correct)

Date –   the payment date

Chq No: -   write here 'DD' if paid by direct debit or cheque number if paid by cheque

Amount -   the value of the payment being made to the supplier. It can be payment in full of outstanding invoice, part payment of outstanding invoice or payment on account of account balance

Allocate the payment to the invoices shown on the screen by entering the payment against the value as stated above.

(Don't forget to SAVE).

c. Printing supplier remittance

Here is how to print supplier payment remittances.

Click on bank accounts then the Remittance button ![Remittances] to print a remittance. (Make sure that you have your remittance stationery in the printer). Select the layout you require and click the Run button.

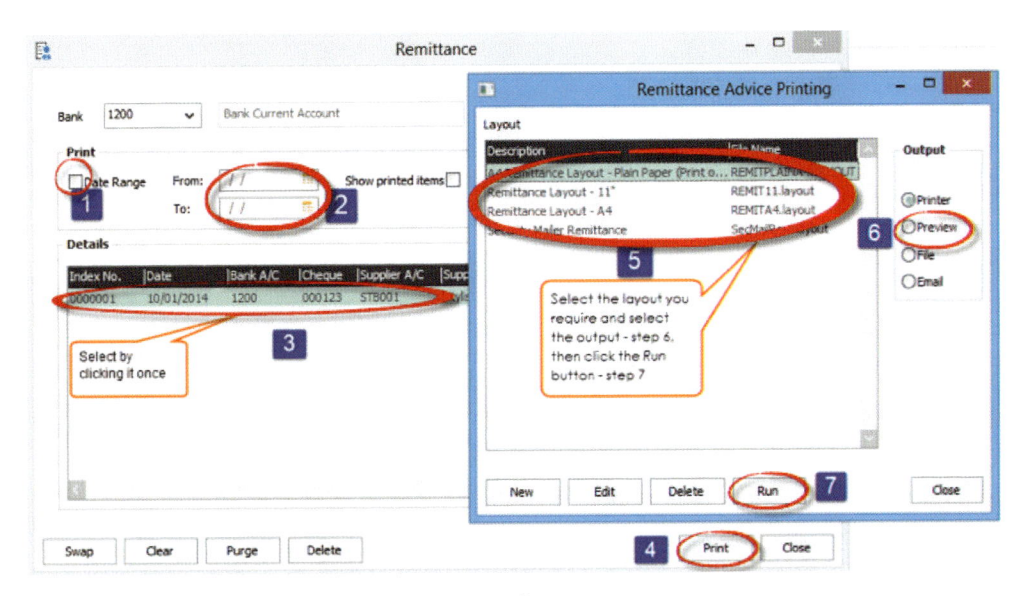

fig. 68

After step 7 in the figure above, a copy of the remittance(s) will appear on the screen. Check how the remittance looks on screen, if it is correct then print it out.

- *Print remittances for each supplier payment showing the cheque number or 'BACS' as the reference.*
- *Enter a pencil tick by the amount posted on the BACS form or cheque book stub*
- *Once the BACS form has been approved and signed fax it to the bank and then file it in the bank transactions file. If it is cheques, once they have been approved and signed attach them to the relevant remittances.*
- *Give all the remittances (including those with cheques attached) to the receptionist to post to the suppliers.*

TASK 11

Processing non-credit transaction payments including payroll postings

All payments out that are not part of supplier payments should be analysed to the correct "nominal/ledger code" before being posted.

Click on Bank accounts then highlight Bank Current account (1200), then Click on Bank payment

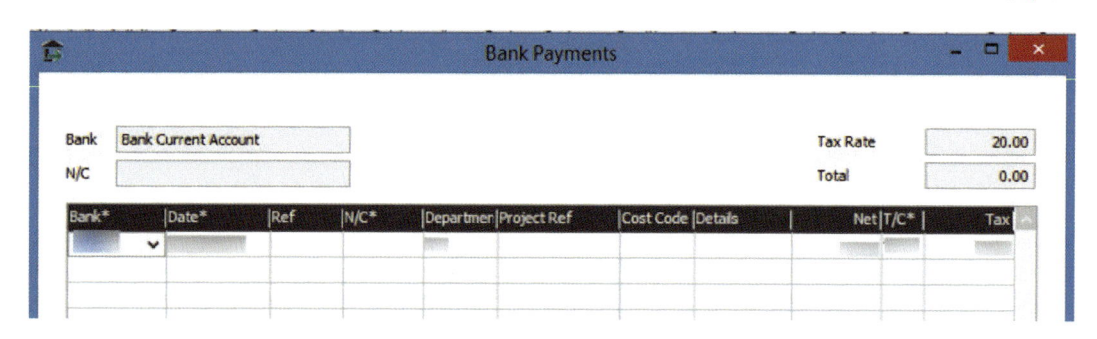

fig. 69

For each payment enter:

Bank – Bank Account number

Date – date of payment per bank statement

Ref – 'payment reference

N/C – the nominal code for that type of purchase (e.g. 7502 for office stationery)

Dept – the department reference number (if applicable)

Details – any description you would find useful

Net – the net amount

T/C – Usually T0 or T2 (Zero rated or exempt)

Tax – the VAT on the sale (this is calculated by Sage automatically but should be nil if there has been no VAT invoice received)

The total of the Net plus VAT should equal the value of the payment. Click SAVE.

Wages Posting Document

Description	Sage N/Code	Debit	Credit
Dr Gross Pay (Gross pay due to employees)			
Dr Gross Pay (Gross pay due to Directors)			
Dr Gross Pay (Statutory Maternity Pay /Sick Pay unrecoverable)			
Dr Gross Pay (or Dr Employers NIC if kept separate)			
Dr Gross Pay (Or Dr Directors Employers NIC if separate)			
Dr Pension Costs (Employers contributions)			
Cr Net Pay Control			
Cr PAYE/NIC Control (Tax deducted)			
Cr PAYE/NIC Control (Employees NI)			
Cr PAYE/NIC Control (Employers NI)			
Cr Pension Fund Liability (Er's/Ee's conts payable)			
Cr Other Deductions			
TOTAL		0	0
	Batch No___		

TASK 12

Setting up recurring entries – standing orders & direct debits

You normally set up recurring entries for things like standing orders and direct debit that the business pays on set days recurrently every month or week.

Say for example rent of £3,000 is to be paid by direct debit every month, here is how you might set up this recurring transaction in Sage 50 accounts.

Click on bank accounts > select the bank account you want the recurring entry to come out from, e.g 1200 (single click on it to select) > then click on recurring items – see below.

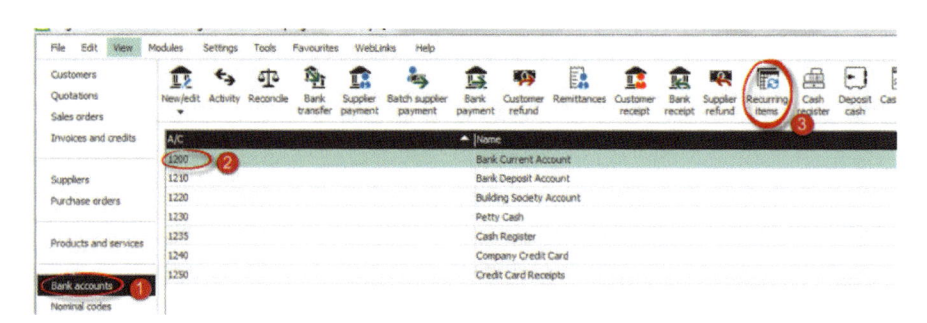

fig. 70

Once you click on recurring items (step 3 in the figure above) a recurring items window similar to the one below will appear.

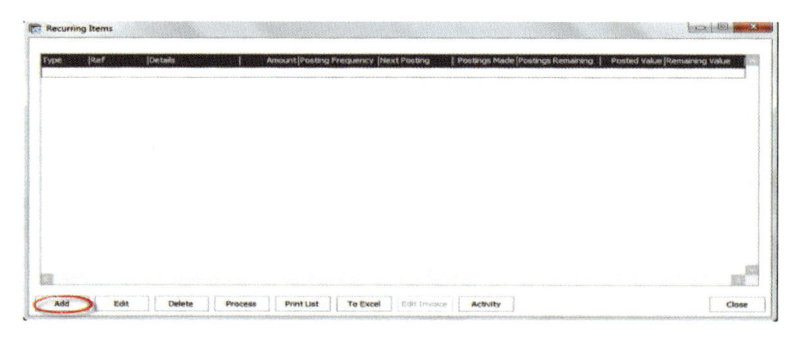

fig. 71

Click on Add as illustrated in the figure above to begin setting up the new recurring entry.

A window similar to the one below will appear once you click Add. Notice how it will be filled out;

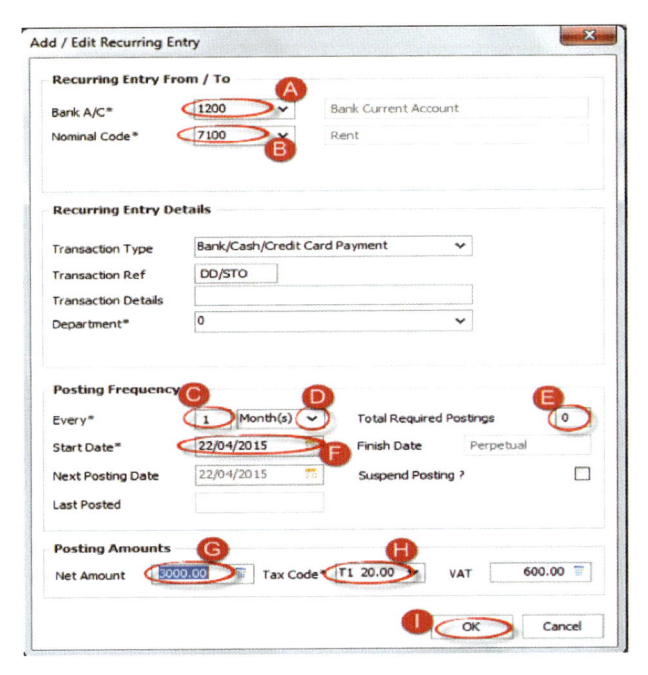

fig. 72

Steps:

A. This is the bank account where the recurring entry will be posted from – e.g. Bank current a/c 1200

B. This is the expense nominal code for the recurring entry (in this case – 7100 for Rent)

C. Frequency of the recurring entry

D. Frequency period of the recurring entry

E. This is the total number of recurring entries required, 0 means the recurring entries are perpetual

F. This is the start date of the recurring entry

G. This is the net amount of the recurring entry

H. This is the tax rate to be used against the net amount of the recurring entry

I. Click OK to finish the setup of recurring entry

Once you click OK – step I above, you will see a window similar to the one below.

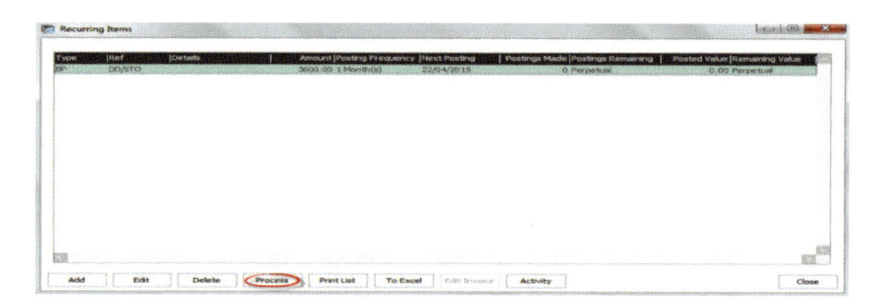

fig. 73

To process the recurring item shown in the figure above, click on process – see figure above.

Here is the window you will see once you click process – see below.

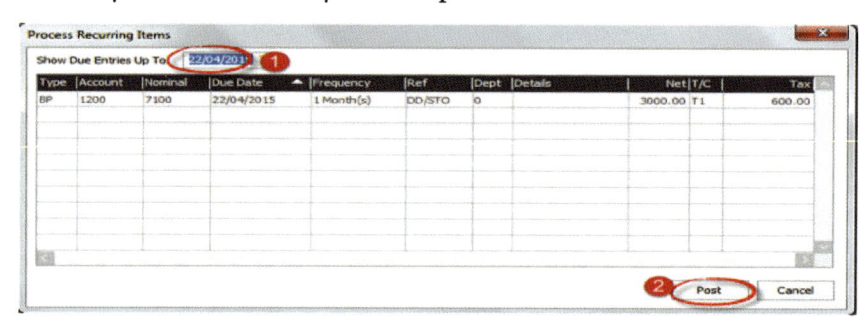

fig. 74

Steps:

1. select the date required for posting

2. click post

Next time you login onto Sage 50 Accounts having recurring entries set up, if that recurring entry is due to be posted on the date you logon, you will see a window similar to the one below asking whether you would like to post the recurring entry(ies).

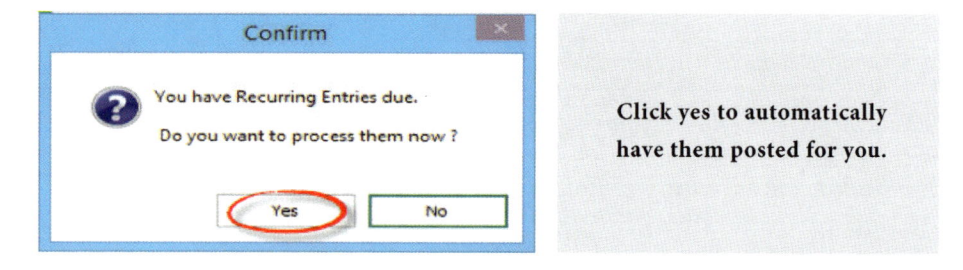

Click yes to automatically have them posted for you.

fig. 75

SECTION 2 - PURCHASE LEDGER

TASK 13

Dealing with petty cash transactions

Businesses generally keep small amounts of cash to meet small miscellaneous payments such as entertainment expenses and stationery costs. Such payments are generally handled by a petty cash imprest system whereby an amount of 'Float' is fixed (say £250). This is the maximum amount of cash that can be held at any time and each time cash level runs low, the petty cash imprest is injected with cash by drawing cash from the bank.

The amount of reimbursement is equal to the expenses paid through petty cash since the time of last reimbursement. Petty cash balance after reimbursement reverts back to the level of the float (in this case £250).

Let's see how we post this entry in Sage 50 Accounts after you have withdrawn money from the bank for petty cash reimbursement.

Click on bank accounts in Sage, then click on Bank transfer then enter the details as shown below.

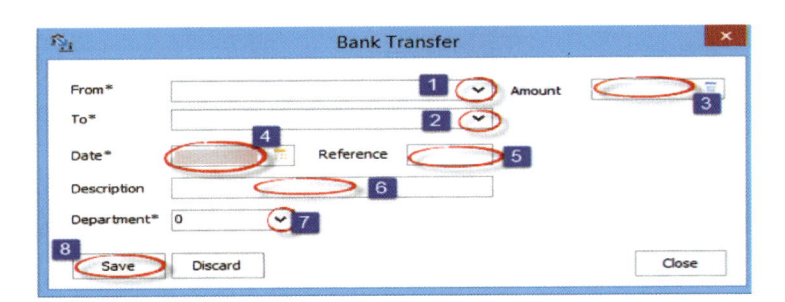

fig. 76

1. On the Account From: - Choose Bank Current Account (1200) from the drop down list of accounts

2. On the Account to:- Choose Bank Petty Cash Account (1230) from the drop down list of Accounts

3. For the Amount section: - type in the amount on petty cash reconciliation report to be reimbursed

4. For Date: - this is the date the money is being cashed from the bank

5. On Ref: - Type in here the word Transfer

6. Description: - write in here the words "Petty cash reimbursement"

7. On Dept.: - put the department number (if applicable)

8. Remember to click Save

Any money taken from the petty cash tin should be replaced with a petty cash voucher. This states what the money was taken for and who took it. The voucher should be signed by the financial accountant or designated signatory.

Whenever a voucher is completed, it is good practice for the custodian to immediately update the petty cash book by adding the amount, type, and date of the expenditure and updating the running cash balance.

For example, if you got some refreshments for the office, e.g. some sweets and you need to be reimbursed the amount you spent, you would need to fill out a petty cash voucher.

Here is how to enter the payments into Sage 50 accounting software for the amount spent out of the petty cash account.

First code each expense with the right nominal analysis code, then click on Bank accounts, after which, select the petty cash account – 1230 by highlighting it (single click on it).

There after click on ![Bank payment]

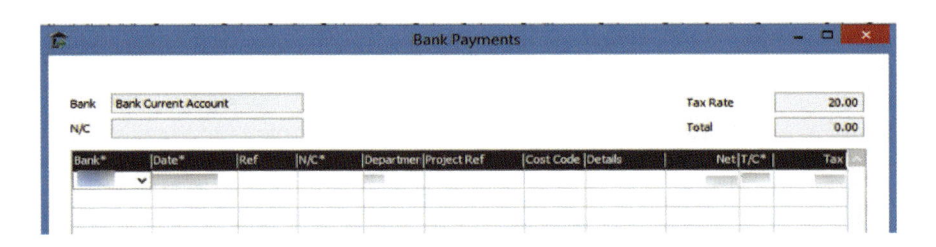

fig. 77

For each payment enter:

Bank* –   Petty Cash Account number - 1230

Date* –   date of petty cash voucher

Ref –   reference per the petty cash voucher

N/C* –   the nominal code for that type of purchase (e.g. 7502 for office stationery or 8205 for coffee)

Dept. – the department reference number (if applicable)

Details – any description you would find useful

Net – the net amount

T/C – Usually T0 or T1 (Zero rated or standard rated)

Tax – the VAT on the sale (this is calculated by Sage automatically but usually it shall be nil if there has been no VAT invoice received). The total of the Net plus VAT should equal the value of stated in the petty cash voucher

Remember to click SAVE. Enter a pencil tick by the amount posted on the petty cash voucher once entered.

> "Sell well, invoice on time, collect money on time and you will do well with your business"
>
> *–Sterling Libs*

SECTION 3

SALES LEDGER

TASK 14

Processing or recording customer invoices

There are two ways you can process or record customer invoices on to Sage 50 Accounts software.

- Option 1: Via customer invoices and credits tab or
- Option 2: Via customer batch invoice

Let's look at option 1 – see illustration below. Please note that this option requires that you should have already recorded your products and services onto Sage 50 already.

Option 1: Via customer invoices and credits tab or

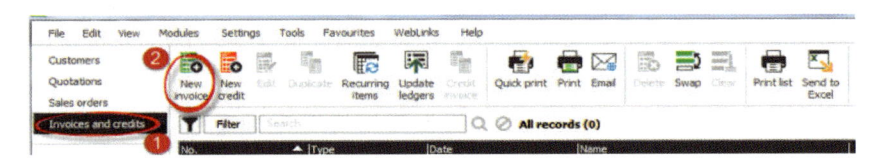

fig. 78

When you click on new invoice (step 2 in figure above) a window similar to the one below will appear, follow the inset steps to record the invoice.

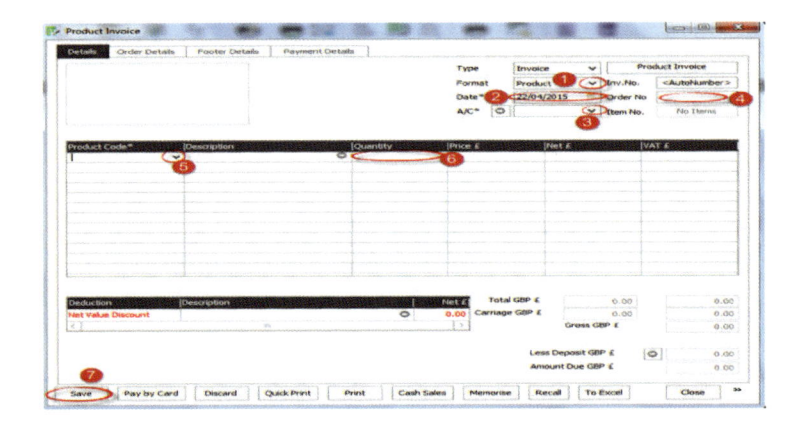

fig. 79

Once you click Save (step 7 in the figure above) the saved invoice will be saved on the invoice & credits records waiting to be posted to the ledgers later.

It can be posted to the ledgers by highlighting that invoice and clicking update – see illustration below:

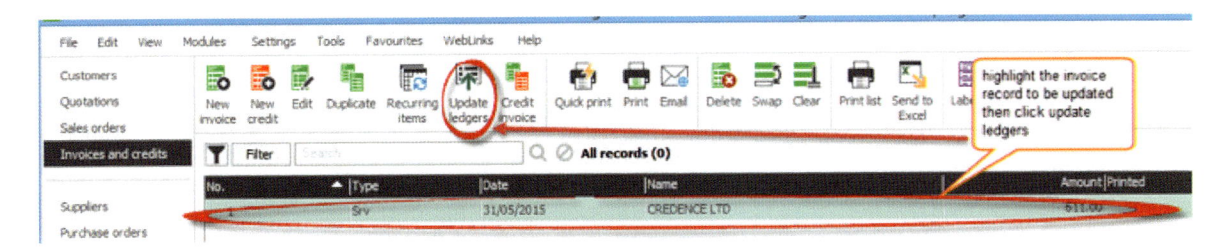

fig. 80

Option 2: recording invoice via customer batch invoice

Click on customers, then click on batch invoice – see illustration in *Fig. 81*

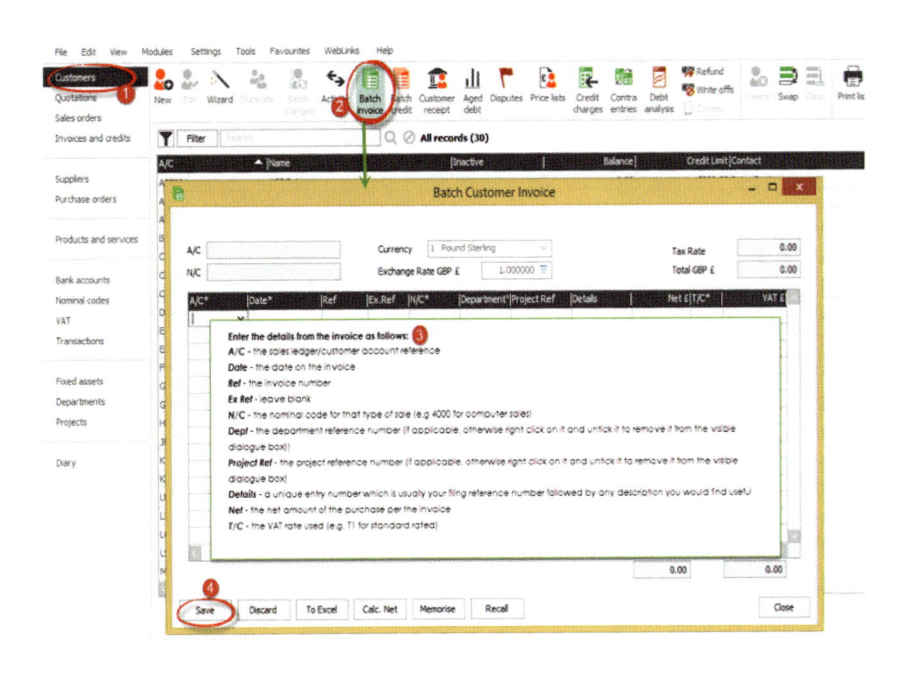

fig. 81

TASK 15

Processing customer credit notes.

Procedure for entry of sales credit notes onto sage.

i. Click on Customers > batch credit and fill out the window asper the instructions in the text box in Fig. 82:

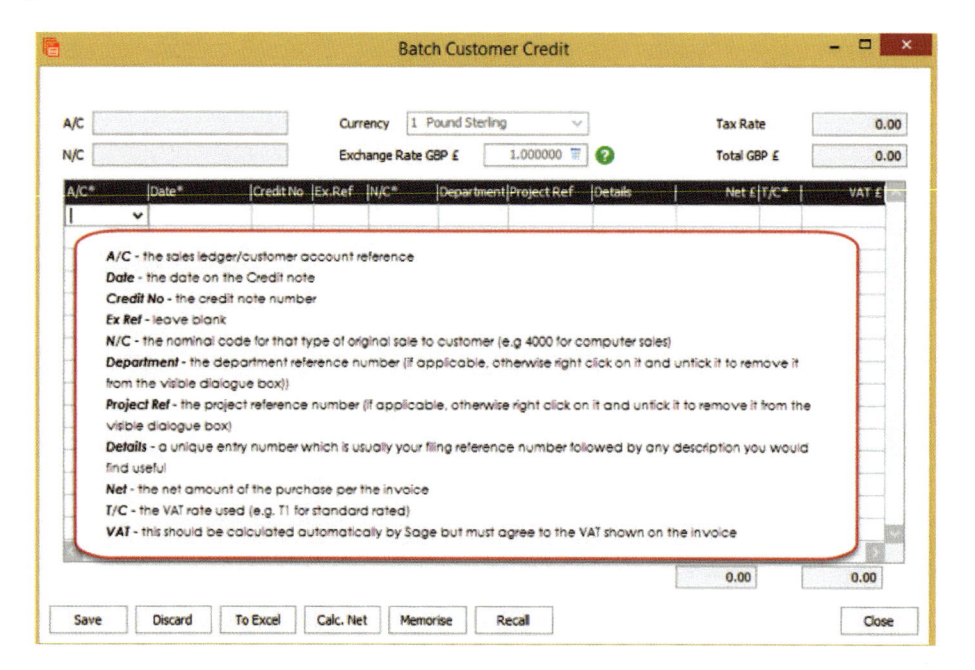

fig. 82

SECTION 3 - SALES LEDGER

TASK 16

Processing customer receipts

Click on Bank accounts, then highlight Bank Current Bank account - 1200 (single click on it), then click on **Customer receipt** or click on customers and then click on **Customer receipt**

A customer receipt – bank current account window will appear – see *Fig. 83*

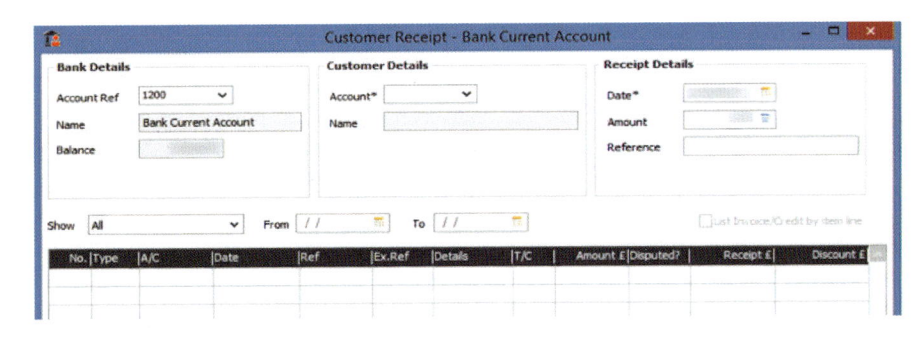

fig. 83

For each customer receipt enter:

A/C – the sales ledger/customer reference

Name – this should come up automatically – but should be checked

Date – date of receipt of the money from customer

Ref – reference of invoice being paid

Amount – amount paid by customer

Allocate the receipt to the invoices shown on the screen as follows;

- ✓ *Payment of outstanding invoice in full (pay in full)*
- ✓ *Part payment of outstanding invoice*

And don't forget to SAVE. *Payment of account*

If you can't find matching invoices to allocate the receipt to, post the receipt as a receipt on account by clicking save without having allocated the receipt.

61

TASK 17

Processing non customer receipts - From Cash register – Cash & Cheque

When a sale is made and Cash or cheque is received, you can enter this transaction in to Sage by clicking on Bank accounts then cash register as illustrated below:

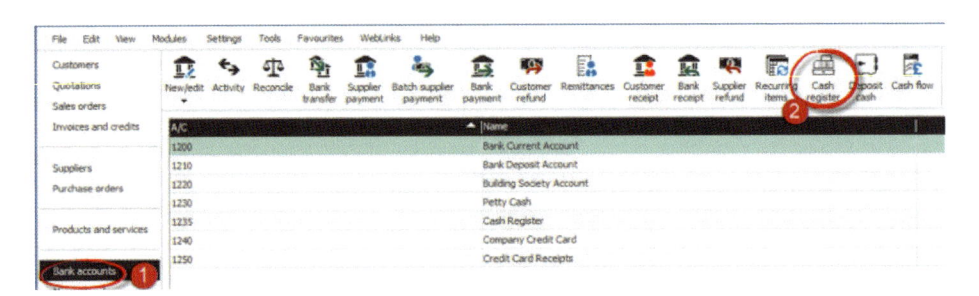

fig. 84

Once you click on cash register as illustrated above, a figure similar to the one below will appear.

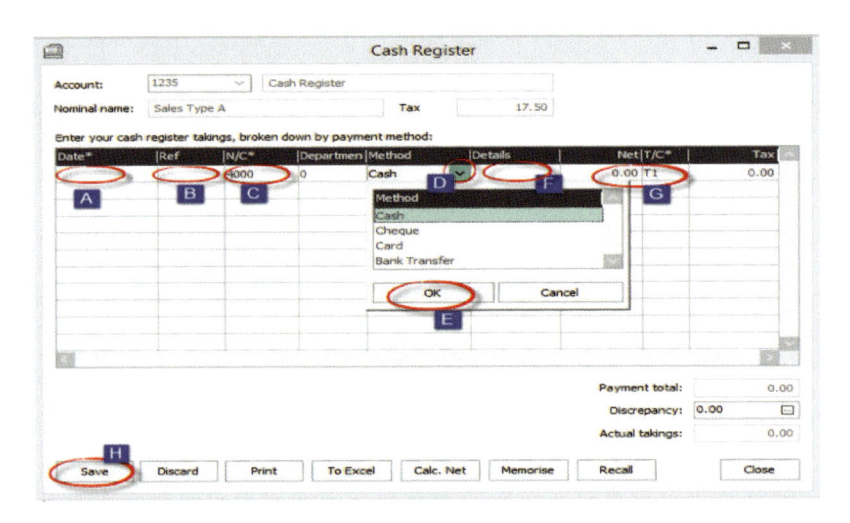

fig. 85

A. Write here the date the sale was made and the cash/cheque received

B. Write the reference for the transaction

C. Write here the nominal code for the sales item sold

D. Click on the drop down arrow to select the mode of receipt of the sale (Cash, Cheque or bank transfer) if it is cheque, write the cheque number on reference in B above

E. Remember to click Ok after selecting the either cash, cheque or bank transfer

F. Write the details of what was sold or any other description that suites the transaction made

G. Write the net amount and the tax code (for VAT rate) of the product or service sold

H. Don't forget to click Save

Repeat this process for as many cash/cheque transactions received for the sales to non-registered customers.

Recording deposits of Cash/Cheque from the Cash register.

Every once in a while, the cash/cheques in the cash register should be deposited to the bank. Depending on what the company's policy for banking cash & cheque receipts is, this can be every day, every 2 days in a week or just once on a specific day of the week. Whatever the day or time, the cash/cheques deposited to the bank from the cash register must have a record of that happening and here is how to record it.

Click on Bank accounts, then click on deposit cash.

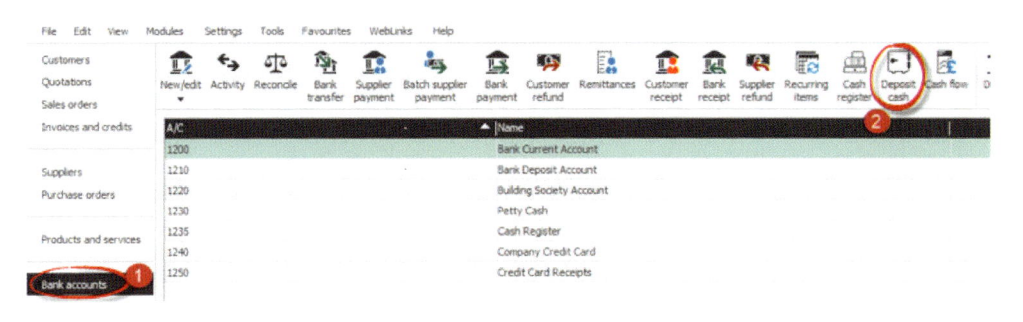

fig. 86

Once you click on deposit cash as illustrated in the figure above (number 2), a window similar to the one below will appear with a record of all the transactions to be cleared to the bank current account once the cash & cheques have been physically taken and deposited to the bank current account.

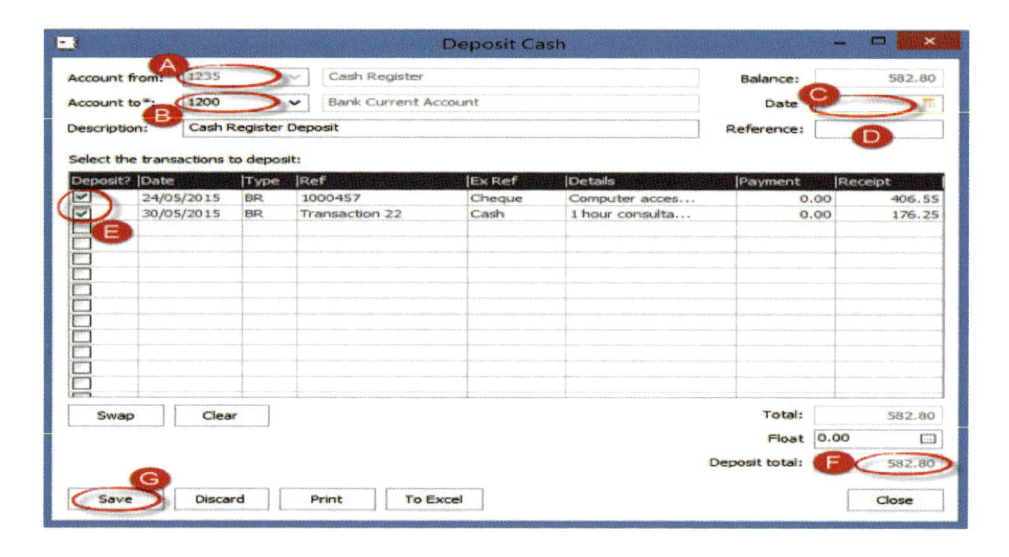

fig. 87

A. The money is being moved from the cash register account – 1235 to

B. The bank current account – 1200

C. Write here the date the money was taken and deposited to the bank current account

D. You can write here a reference e.g. the name of the person who did the banking that day

E. Just tick the record of the transactions whose money is being deposited into the bank account

F. Notice that as you tick in E, the figure in F appears

G. Don't forget to Save

You have now completed recording the cash/cheque deposit in to the Bank current account.

TASK 18

Processing non customer receipts - From Bank Statement – Cash/Cheque/BACs

Bank receipts are a quick and easy way to record one off receipts or receipts which aren't from a customer, such as interest, dividends received, money received for an insurance claim or for a grant.

When you post a bank receipt the transaction type changes depending on the bank account type in the bank record. The receipts appear on the audit trail as the following transaction types:

> BR = Receipts from a bank account.
>
> CR = Receipts from a cash account.
>
> VR = Receipts from a credit card account.

To post a bank receipt from the bank statement, click on Bank accounts then Bank receipt. See figure below.

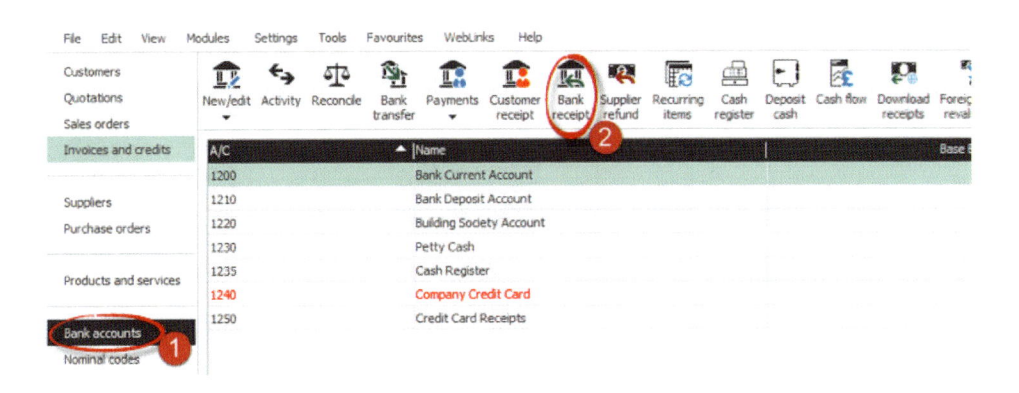

fig. 88

After clicking Bank receipts (step 2 in the figure above) a window similar to *Fig. 89* will appear.

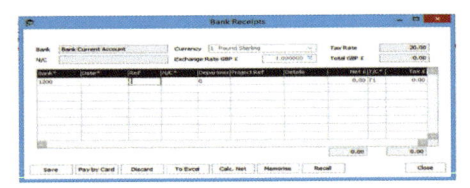

fig. 89

Complete the window as follows:

Bank* -	From the drop-down list, choose the bank account you want to receive the money.
Date* -	Enter the date of the receipt.
Ref -	Enter the reference you want to associate with the receipt.
N/C* -	From the drop-down list, choose the required nominal code.
Fund - Company	This only appears if you select Enable Charity\Non-Profit in Settings > Preferences > Parameters.
	From the drop-down list, choose the required fund
Project Ref - and	This only appears if you select Enable Project Costing in Settings > Company Preferences > Parameters. This option is available on Sage 50 Accounts Plus Accounts Professional only.
	From the drop-down list, choose the required project.
Details -	Enter the details for the receipt.
Net - Calc.	Enter the net value of the receipt. Tip: If you enter the gross value and click Net, the net and tax values calculate based on the tax code.
T/C* -	From the drop-down list, choose the required tax code.
Tax -	This automatically calculates from the net value and tax code.

SECTION 4

DOUBLE ENTRY REVIEW

TASK 19

Double entry and journals review

Using double entry principles, record the following transactions:

a. Cash Sale of £700 inclusive of VAT at 20%; £450 was paid by cash & £250 by bank transfer

DR	Cash	CR
700		

DR	Sales	CR
	583.33	

DR	VAT on Sales.	CR
	116.67	

b. Credit sale of 854.25 inclusive of 20% VAT and 2 days later goods worth £250 were returned

DR	Receivables	CR
854.25		250

DR	Sales	CR
208.33		711.87

DR	VAT on Sales.	CR
41.67		142.37

c. Cash Purchase for the business for £1,850.78 inclusive of VAT at 20% using Directors own funds

DR	Director loan a/c	CR
		1850.78

DR	Purchase	CR
1542.32		

DR	VAT on purchases	CR
308.46		

d. Invoice received from British gas of £255.76 inclusive of 5% VAT

DR	British Gas	CR
		255.76

DR	Gas	CR
243.58		

DR	VAT on purchases	CR
12.18		

e. Using journal entry, record the following transactions and enter them into the computer

i. Cash purchase of computer for £450 plus 20% VAT on 22/03/20XX for Sales manager and

ii. Director buys an iPad worth £478 inclusive of 20% VAT for personal use on 30/03/20XX using company bank card

Date	Account	Ref	Description	Debit	Credit
22/03/20XX	0030	SM	Computer for Sales manager	450	
22/03/20XX	2201	SM	Computer for Sales manager	90	
22/03/20XX	1200	SM	Computer for Sales manager		540
30/03/20XX	2301	DL	Director loan (iPad purchase)	478	
30/03/20XX	1200	DL	Director loan (iPad purchase)		478

Journal Entry in Sage 50

Journals can be used to transfer balances between nominal codes. They can also be used to correct balances as they don't affect customer or supplier accounts.

Journal transactions are always posted with an equal value in the Debit and Credit columns, with at least one journal debit and one journal credit per journal posting. You can't delete a journal, you must reverse them instead – see Task 20.

To post a journal, click on Nominal Codes then Journal entry as illustrated in the figure below.

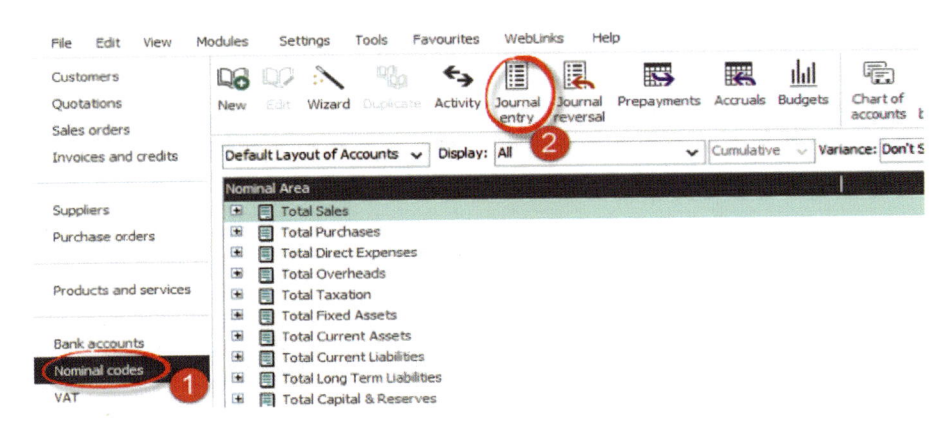

fig. 90

After clicking journal entry as illustrated in step 2 in the figure above, a window similar to *Fig. 91* will appear.

THE ACCOUNTS ASSISTANT JOB MANUAL

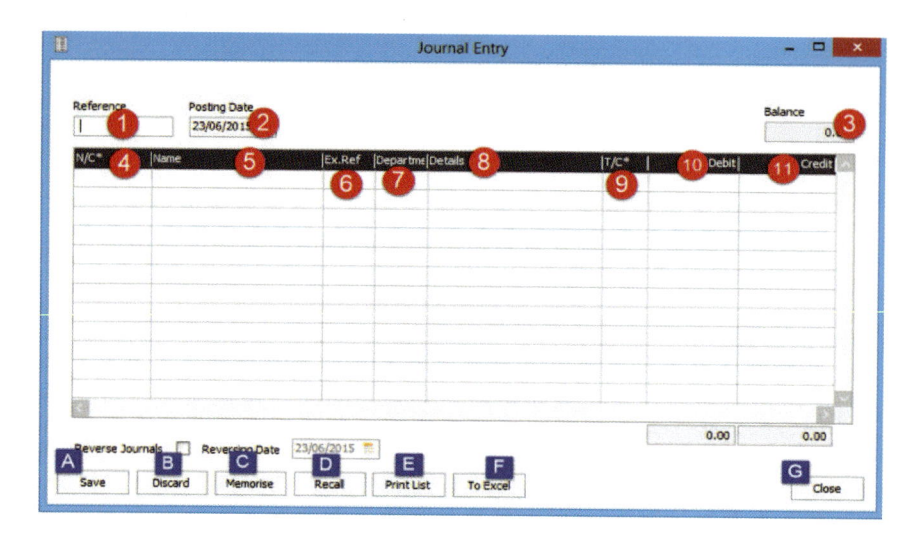

fig. 91

You can then check or enter the information in journal as below.

1. Reference – Write here the reference for the journal, up to 30 characters only.

2. Posting date – Write here the date you want to use to post the journal.

3. Balance - This is the difference between the total of debit (10) and credit (11) values for the journal. Please note that before you can save the journal the balance must be zero, otherwise the journal will not be saved – there will be a warning message on the screen to call your attention to this fact.

4. N/C* - Type in here or select from the drop down list the nominal account code you want to affect this part of the transaction

5. Name – This is the name of the nominal account code you have entered in 4 above and it will appear automatically, you don't have to type it in.

6. Ex.Ref – You can type in here an additional reference to further identify the journal, up to 30 characters are allowed.

7. Department – Select from the drop down list the department number for the transaction.

8. Details – Write in here the description for the transaction, up to 60 characters allowed.

9. T/C* - Type in here or select from the drop down list the appropriate tax code for the transaction.

10. Debit – Enter in here any debit value for the transaction.

11. Credit – Enter in here any credit value for the transaction.

Please note that the overall difference between your debit values & credit values should be equal to zero for you to successfully be able to save the journal.

Complete the journal entry window by clicking one of the following as illustrated in the figure above.

A. Save – Click here to save the journal and create the transactions.

B. Discard – Click here to clear the information you have entered in 1, 4-11.

C. Memorise – Use this to save the details you have entered, so you can recall the information.

D. Recall – Use this to recall any previously memorised journals.

E. Print List – Click here if you want to print the journal.

F. To Excel – Use this to send the information to an Excel spreadsheet.

G. Close – Click here to close the journal window.

TASK 20

Reversing Journals

You should take note of the following about the journals you want to reverse:

- Get the journal numbers or transaction numbers of the journals to be reversed in Sage
- Write down the date the journals were posted and
- The amounts then,
- Back up your work

Now then, with that information, click on Nominal codes, then click on journal reversal – see below.

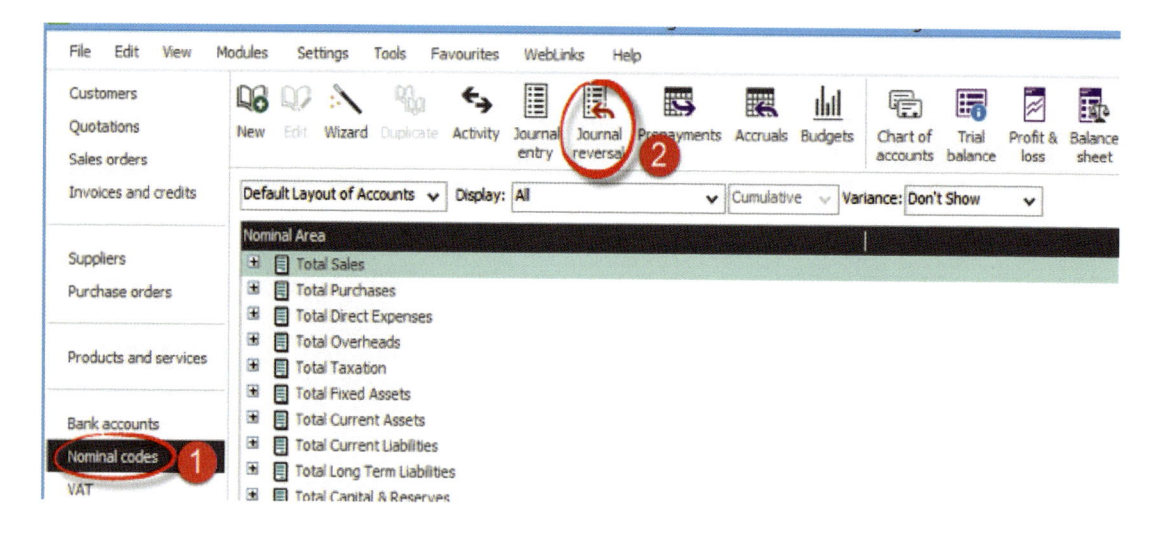

fig. 92

Once you click journal reversal – step 2 in the figure above, a window similar to the one below will appear.

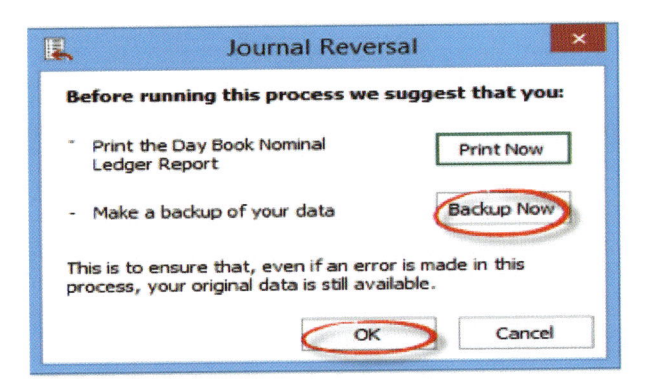

fig. 93

Make a backup of your work if you haven't already done so then click OK.

Once you click OK, a transaction range window similar to *Fig. 94* will appear.

fig. 94

Once you click Ok as illustrated in the figure above, a window similar to the one below will appear (please note that the figures shown here are for examples, your own work will have its own figures which will be different from the ones used here).

73

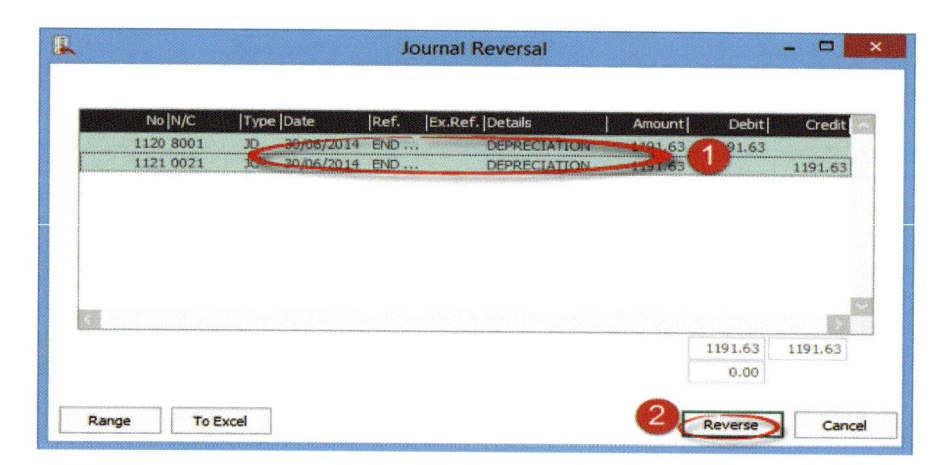

fig. 95

1. Highlight both entries to be reversed and then

2. Click on reverse and a window similar to Fig. 96 will appear

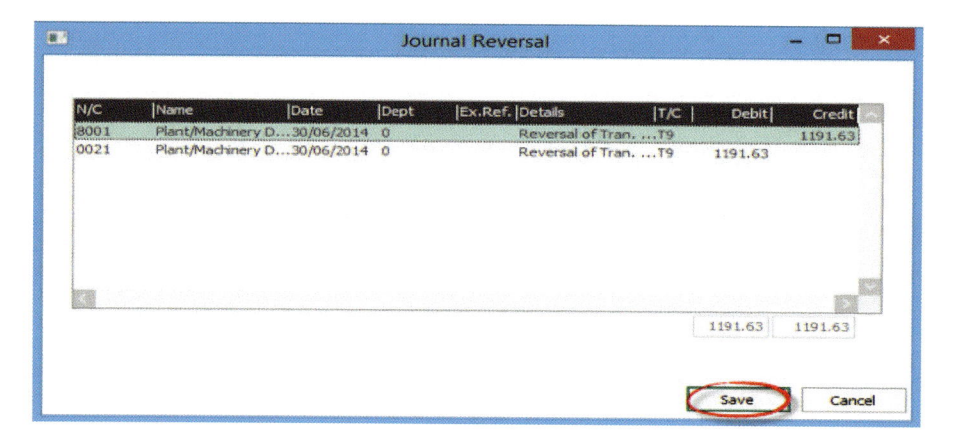

fig. 96

Click save.

If you do not click save, the journal will not be reversed.

If at this point you realise that you were not meant to reverse the journal, just click cancel and cancel again in both windows.

SECTION 5
RECONCILIATIONS

TASK 21

VAT return preparation, reconciliation & submission to HMRC

a. Checklist

Before starting your VAT return process, go through the VAT return checklist (see below, making sure that everything has been done).

Step	Description	Tick
i	Has all output tax been traced to sales invoices or Daily Income sheets and invoices?	☐
ii	Has all output tax been declared at the correct VAT rate?	☐
iii	Has all input tax been traced to purchase invoices and petty cash vouchers?	☐
iv	Has all input tax been claimed at the correct VAT rate?	☐
v	Have all bank receipt and bank payment entries been checked to ensure that the correct VAT code has been applied?	☐
vi	Have all bad debts been entered onto the accounting system and the VAT claimed?	☐
vii	Have sales invoices been issued for any asset sales? Has the correct output tax been declared?	☐
viii	Check that no input tax has been claimed for goods for private use	☐

ix	Check that input tax has not been claimed for entertainment (unless it can be proven to be wholly and exclusively a business cost)	☐
x	Has a fuel scale charge been included in the VAT calculation (needed if the company pays ANY private petrol/diesel bills)?	☐
xi	Has only 50% of the input VAT been claimed on any cars that are leased or hired?	☐
xii	If you make exempt supplies have you checked whether the partial exemption rules apply?	☐
xiii	If you import or export goods have all the documentation been kept and recorded and treated correctly for VAT purposes?	☐
xiv	If you have dealt with firms in other countries have you recorded their VAT registration numbers?	☐
xv	Has the nominal code for VAT been checked to ensure that no journals have been entered which would affect the VAT return?	☐
xvi	Have all manual additions been checked?	☐

After successfully going through the checklist above, proceed with the VAT return process set up as below.

b. Select the VAT scheme & setting up e.submission credentials.

When setting up your software it's important to choose the correct VAT scheme for your company.

You can either choose your VAT scheme when you first set up your company or from Settings > Company Preferences >VAT – see *Fig. 97*

THE ACCOUNTS ASSISTANT JOB MANUAL

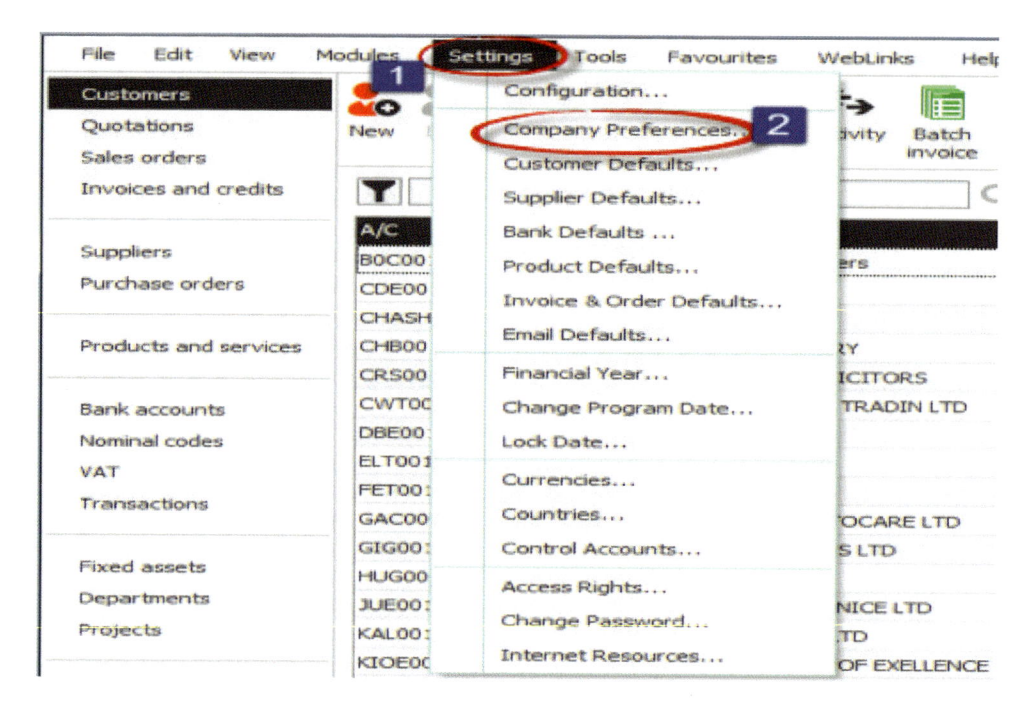

fig. 97

After you have clicked Company preferences, the window as illustrated below will appear.

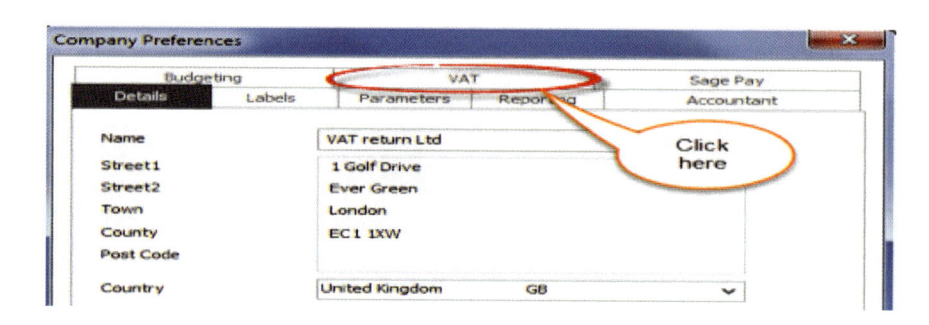

fig. 98

Click on VAT as Illustrated in the figure above and you will notice *Fig. 99*. Fill it out as illustrated (inset illustrations).

SECTION 5 RECONCILIATIONS

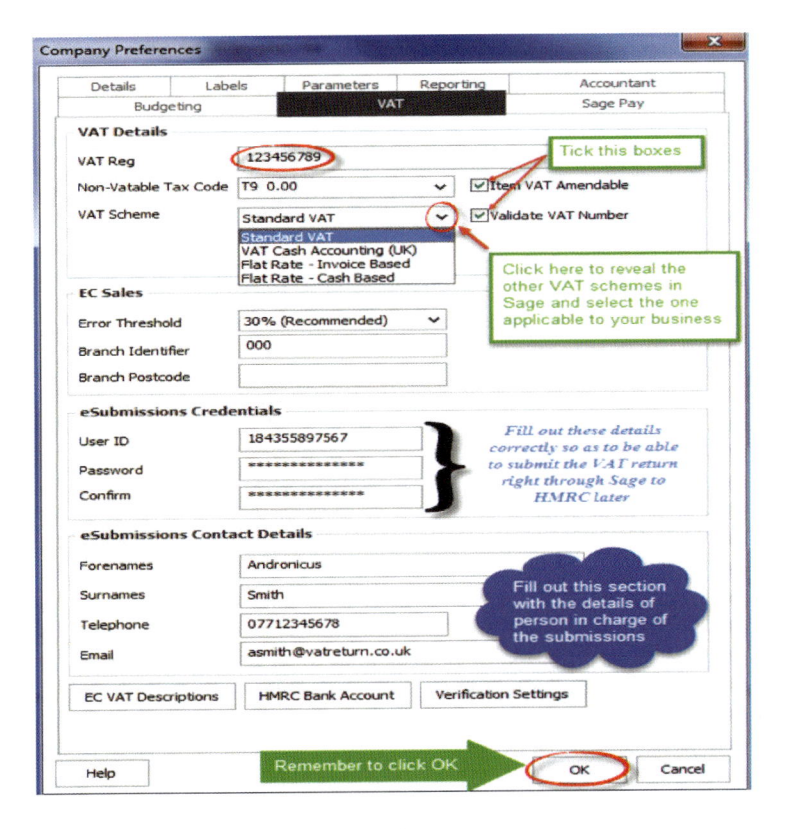

fig. 99

c. Calculate the VAT

After you have clicked OK as shown in the figure above, click on VAT, then VAT return as illustrated in next figure below to calculate the VAT.

fig. 100

The window for the VAT return similar to *Fig. 101* will appear (follow the inset instructions 1-3 to calculate the VAT values).

79

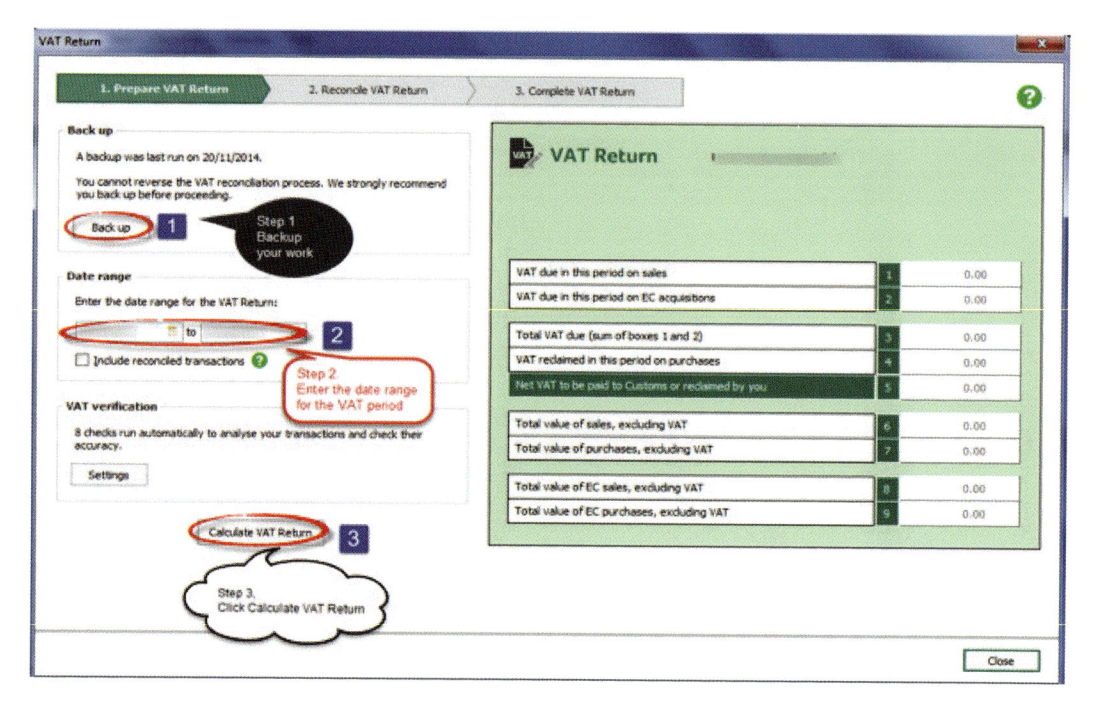

fig. 101

Once you click calculate VAT return (step 3 in the figure above), the following message as below will appear. Click OK to proceed.

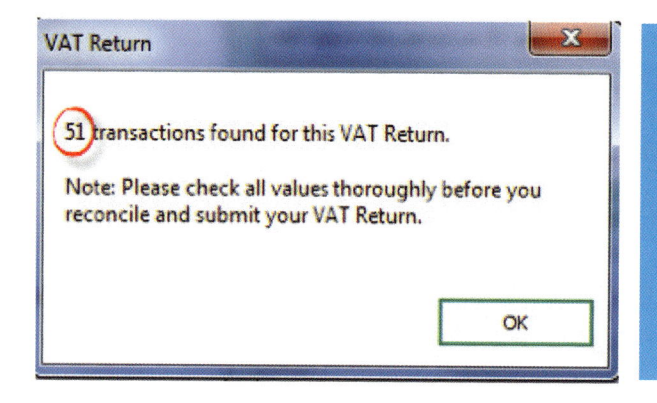

The number 51 circled in the adjacent figure is representative of the number of transactions Sage will find to be used for the VAT return from what you would have entered in to the system. Yours might be different.
Click OK to proceed

fig. 102

Once you click OK, the VAT return will be populated with figures. This figures have been calculated based on a standard VAT scheme.

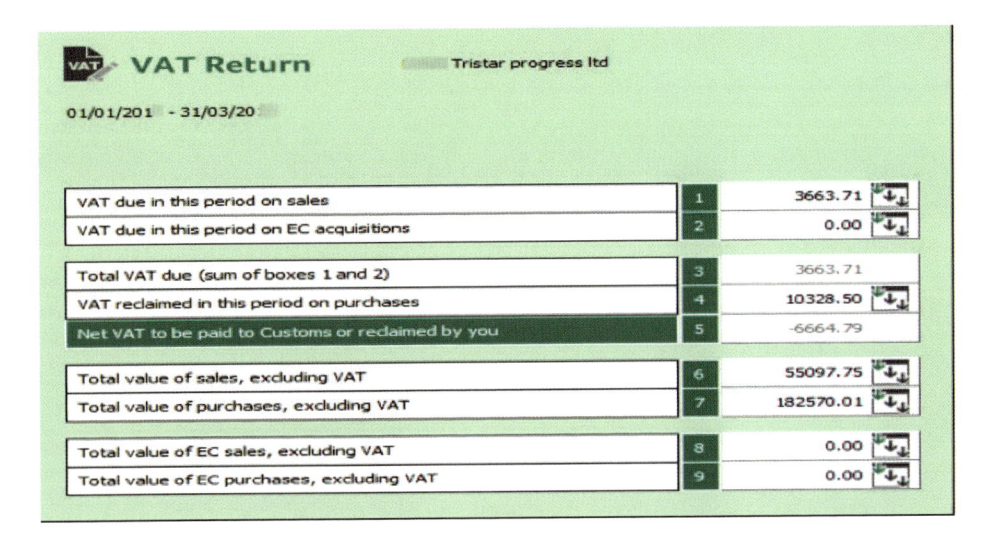

VAT due in this period on sales	1	3663.71
VAT due in this period on EC acquisitions	2	0.00
Total VAT due (sum of boxes 1 and 2)	3	3663.71
VAT reclaimed in this period on purchases	4	10328.50
Net VAT to be paid to Customs or reclaimed by you	5	-6664.79
Total value of sales, excluding VAT	6	55097.75
Total value of purchases, excluding VAT	7	182570.01
Total value of EC sales, excluding VAT	8	0.00
Total value of EC purchases, excluding VAT	9	0.00

fig. 103

d. Reconcile the figures in the VAT return above.

Here is how to do it:

- You need to check the figures in box (1, 4, 6 & 7) to see whether they match figures from your physical records.

To do so, click on the figure in box 1 for example and you will notice that a separate window (A) will appear – see below.

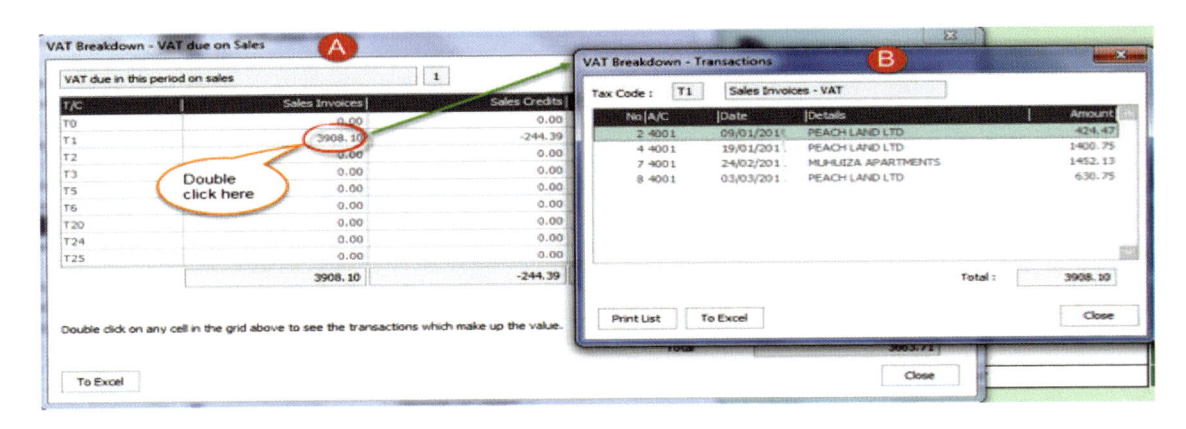

fig. 104

A. Represents the window which first appears when you click on the figure in box 1 of the VAT return.

> It has the figure for VAT from the sales invoices and VAT from credit notes for the return period. Double click on the figure for sales invoices shown here and another window will appear – window B
>
> B. This window appears as a result of double clicking on the value of the VAT on sales invoices on window A and it gives a breakdown of the transactions that constitute the Sales tax (Sales VAT) for the period.

Compare these figures to the figures in the physical records making sure that the figures shown in here (window B) are also in the physical records and vice versa.

Now, in a similar manner, check figures in box 4, 6, & 7.

If the figures match those that you have on the physical records, then, press reconcile VAT button, otherwise make the necessary corrections before clicking reconcile VAT.

See below how to make adjustments of errors in the previous submitted return in this current return.

e. Making adjustments to VAT return for errors in previous returns

If the net value of the errors found on the previous return is between £10,000 and £50,000 but does not exceed 1% of the box 6 (net outputs) VAT return declaration due for the return period in which the errors are discovered, then you can adjust the VAT value in the current return.

Here is how to do it on Sage 50 Accounts. Click on adjustments as illustrated in *Fig. 105*.

SECTION 5 RECONCILIATIONS

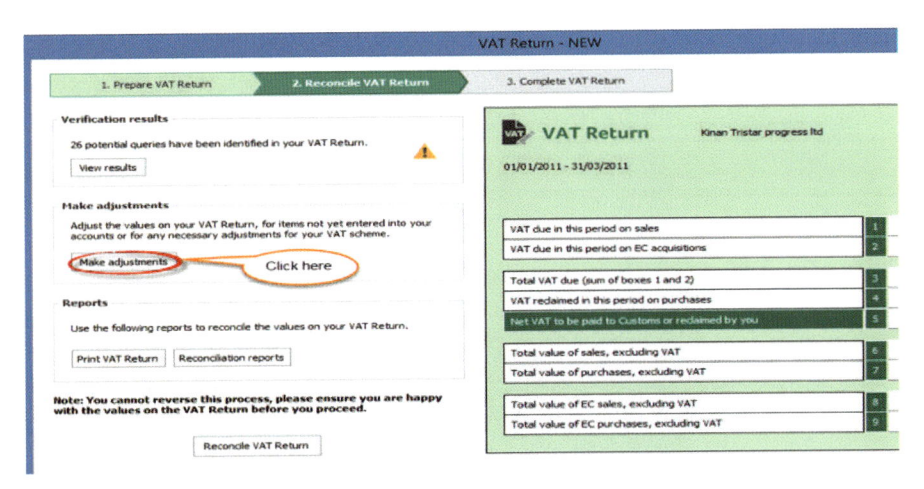

fig. 105

Once you click make adjustments as illustrated in the figure above, a window similar to the one below will appear.

Say for example the error was relating to the VAT on sales in the previous return submitted, follow the inset annotated instructions in the figure below to make the necessary adjustments.

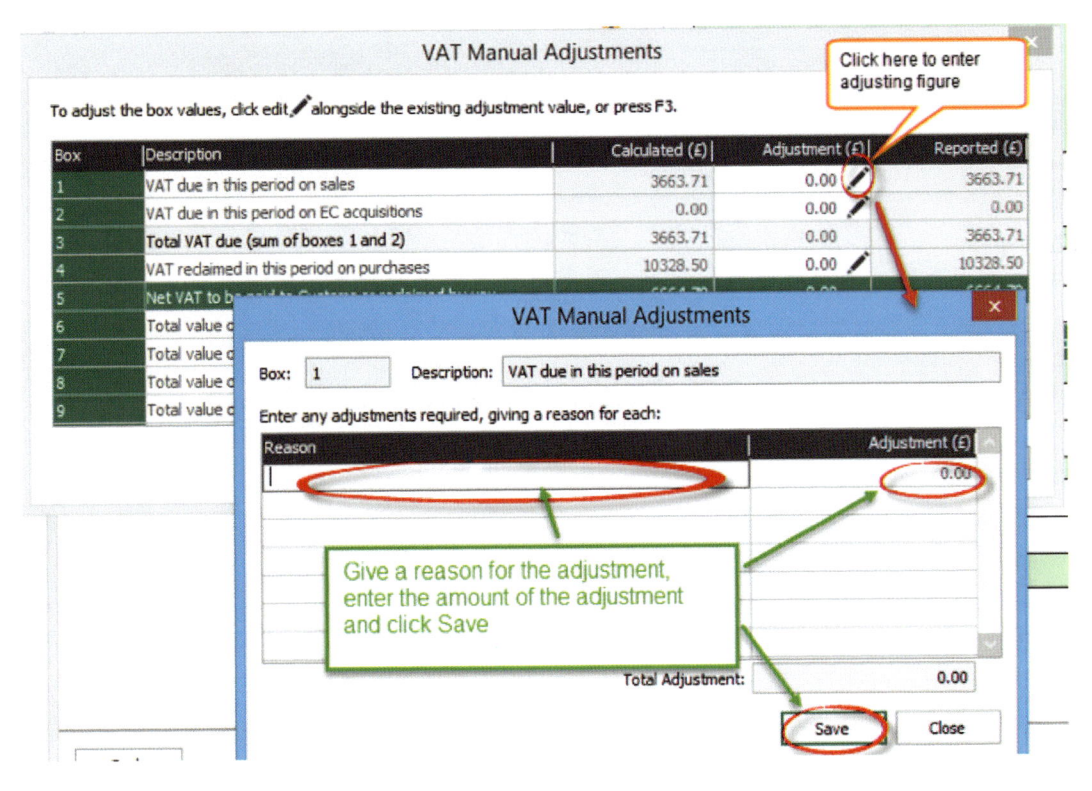

fig. 106

83

THE ACCOUNTS ASSISTANT JOB MANUAL

After clicking save as illustrated in the figure above, Click close on the window that remains and then click reconcile VAT Return after all the figures in the return have been verified to be correct.

Once you click Reconcile VAT, you will see a window similar to the one below ready for you to start printing the VAT reports.

f. Printing the VAT return report

Click print (bottom left hand corner of the VAT return) to print VAT return reconciliation reports .

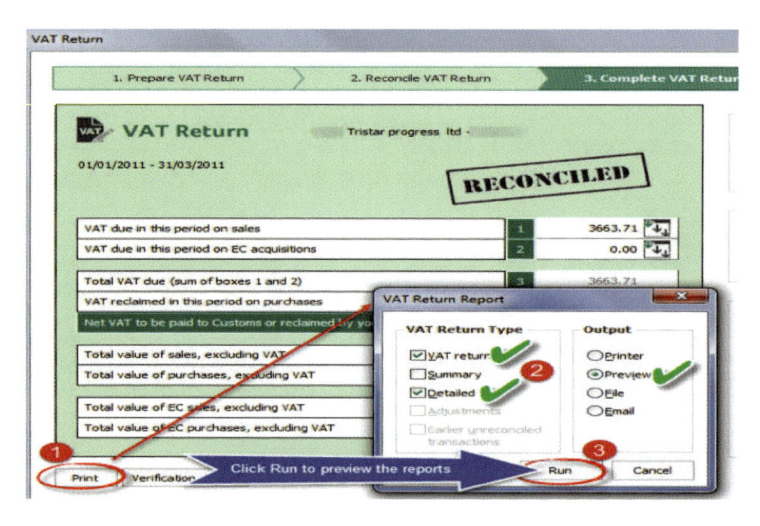

fig. 107

g. Submitting a VAT Return to HMRC from Sage 50 Accounts

Once you have printed the reconciliation reports, you can now submit the VAT return to HMRC from Sage. See step 2 in *Fig. 108*

But before you do make the submission, you will need to make a VAT transfer from the Sales tax control account and purchase tax control account to the VAT liability account. See step 1 in the figure below.

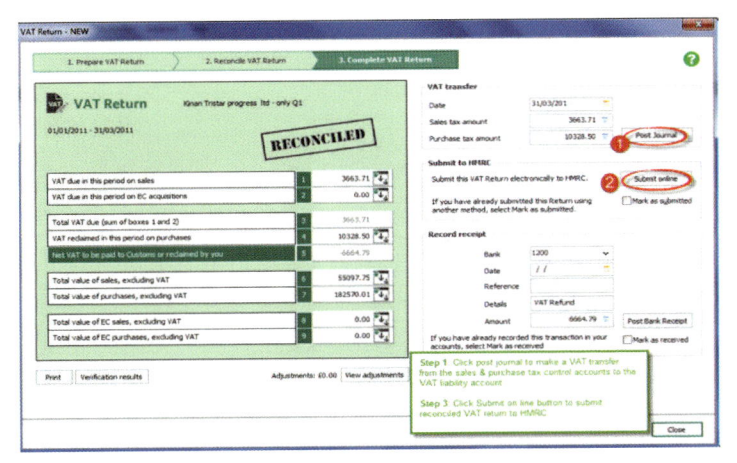

fig. 108

Step 1: *Click post journal to make a VAT transfer from the sales & purchase tax control accounts to the VAT liability account*

Step 2: *Click Submit on line button to submit reconciled VAT return to HMRC*

In step 2 in the above figure, when you click Submit online, a window similar to the one below will appear. Click yes to continue.

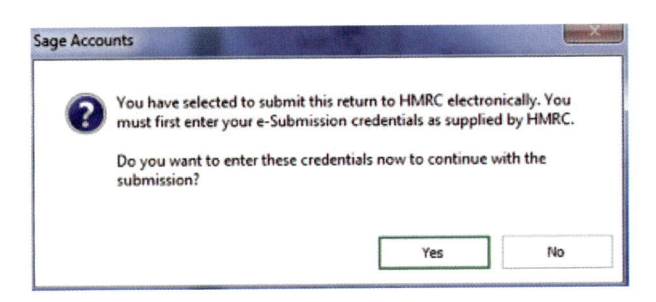

fig. 109

Now, fill in the e.Submission credentials and contact details – as mentioned in the inset instruction (note that the e.Submission credential details would have to be obtained by registering for HMRC online tax services – VAT, and details should have been activated for use before you can use them here).

THE ACCOUNTS ASSISTANT JOB MANUAL

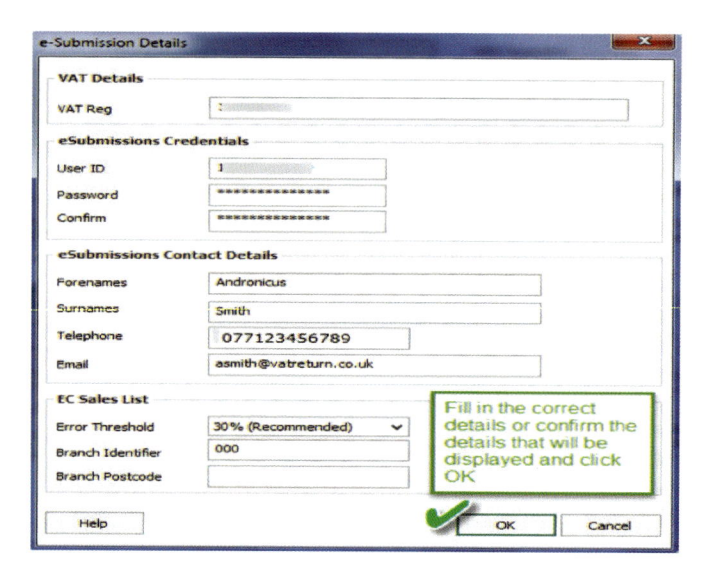

fig. 110

Once you click Ok, Sage will attempt to submit the VAT return to HMRC and will give a report of successful or unsuccessful submission depending on what will happen.

h. Correcting arithmetical errors during your VAT reconciliation process

If you discover that there is an error in one or more of the figures in step d above, correct the error by noting the transaction number of the transaction that has an error. See figure below.

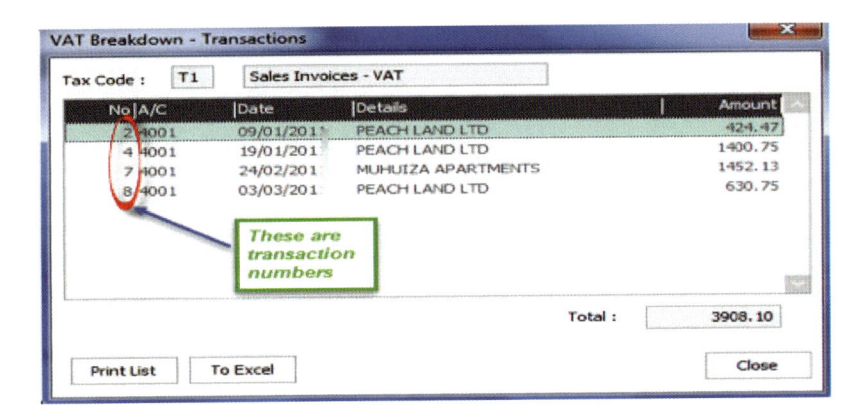

fig. 111

Once you have noted the transaction number of the transaction(s) with an error, close all open VAT return windows and go to transactions tab, click on it and search for the transaction with the error using the search bar (type the transaction number in there and click the search symbol or simply press enter on your key board).

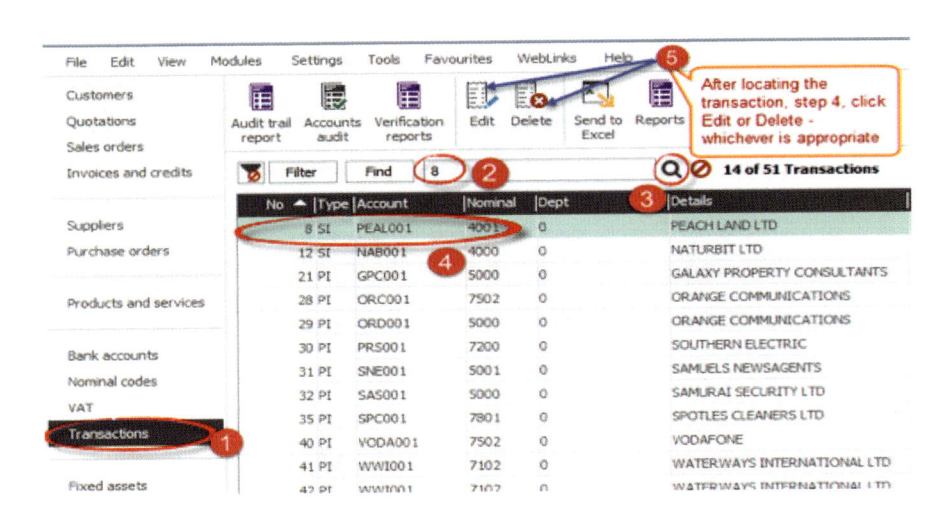

fig. 112

If in step 5 in the figure above, you click Edit, a window with a message for you to confirm your next action will appear, it looks like this:

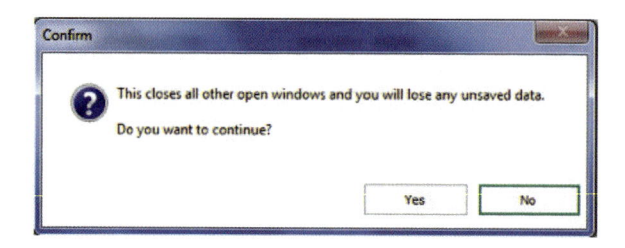

fig. 113

Click yes to continue and the following window will appear. See *Fig. 114*

fig. 114

If you click edit again as illustrated in the figure above, a window similar to *Fig. 115* will appear.

fig. 115

After clicking Close, click Save and go back to your VAT return by clicking VAT > VAT return > put the date range > click calculate VAT, check the figures to see whether the error has been resolved, if so, click on reconcile VAT return.

TASK 22

Performing Bank Reconciliation

Here is how to do it in Sage 50 accounts.

i. Open the Bank module, then choose the account to be reconciled from the list displayed e.g. Current account - 1200.

ii. Follow the sequence of steps shown in the figure below from your Sage 50 software

The Statement Summary window – 4 appears after step 3

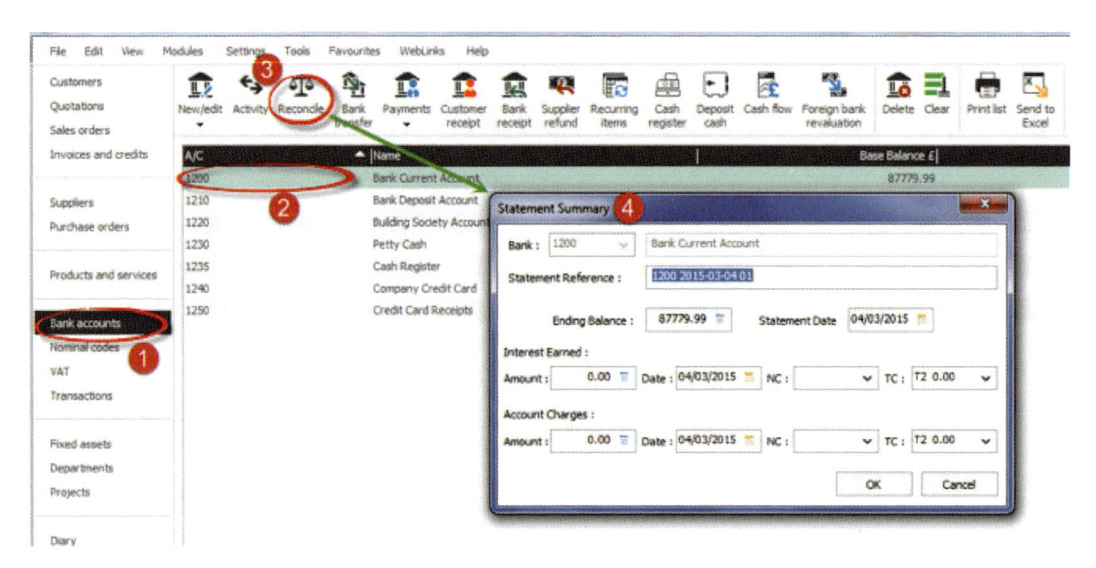

fig. 116

iii. Use the Statement Summary window – number 4 in the figure above to record information shown on your bank statement .i.e. you need to mainly record the ending balance (which should be the balance on your bank statement), statement date and statement reference (all these relate to your bank statement)

iv. When you have entered your statement information, click OK (next to cancel) – bottom right of statement summary window 4.

After clicking OK as mentioned above, the Bank reconciliation window appears, showing the selected account name at the top of the window. See *Fig. 117*

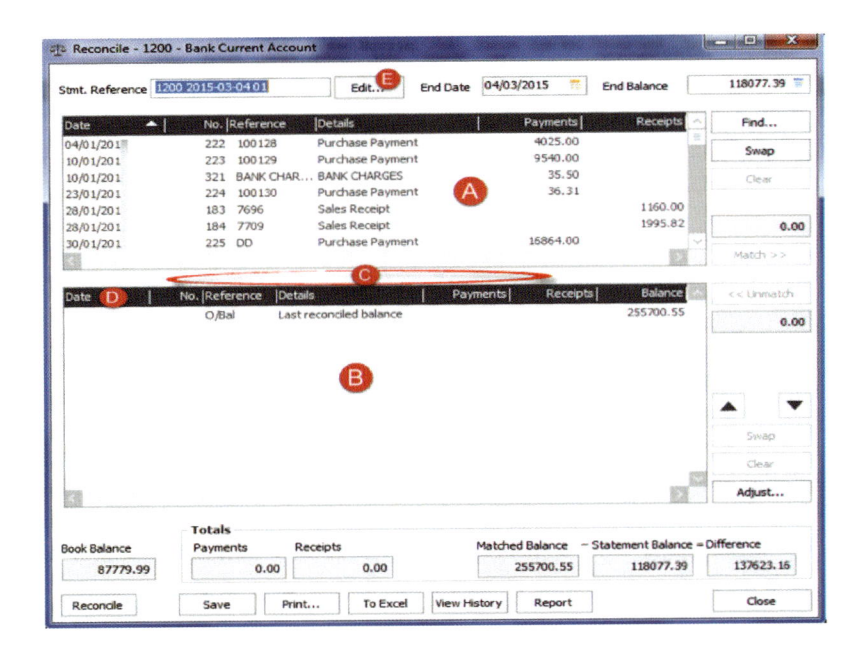

fig. 117

Explanations of the sections (A-E) shown in the figure above:

A. This is the unmatched items section and contains all unreconciled transactions from the cash book, up to and including the Statement (End) date.

B. This is the matched against Statement section. If this is the first time the bank account is to be reconciled the account's opening balance appears as 0, otherwise the reconciled balance from the previous reconciliation appears. It is displayed for information purposes only, it cannot be removed or changed.

C. This is the horizontal splitter bar and it is where you can adjust the height of the upper and lower sections and you do it by dragging it up or down, as required

D. This section is used to configure the columns that can be displayed in both panes (the dark black areas). Simply right click on the column header and select the columns to be displayed from the menu that appears by ticking them or deselect the ones that you don't want to appear by unticking them.

E. You can click here to remove or unmatch any account charges or interests earned that have been recorded using the statement summary window in the preceding section. To remove or unmatch the account charges, simply click on edit – (E in the figure above), then set the charge/interest amount to zero on the displayed statement summary window that will appear and then click OK. Confirm this action by clicking OK when prompted.

Okay, you will now need to have your bank statement at hand because we are going to look at:

i. The reconciliation process.

- *Work through your bank statement, one line at a time beginning from the top of the first page of the bank statement you are reconciling. Match a transaction on your bank statement to a transaction in the Unmatched Items area Section A – see below.*

- *Select the item to be matched, then click Match. – as illustrated in the figure below*

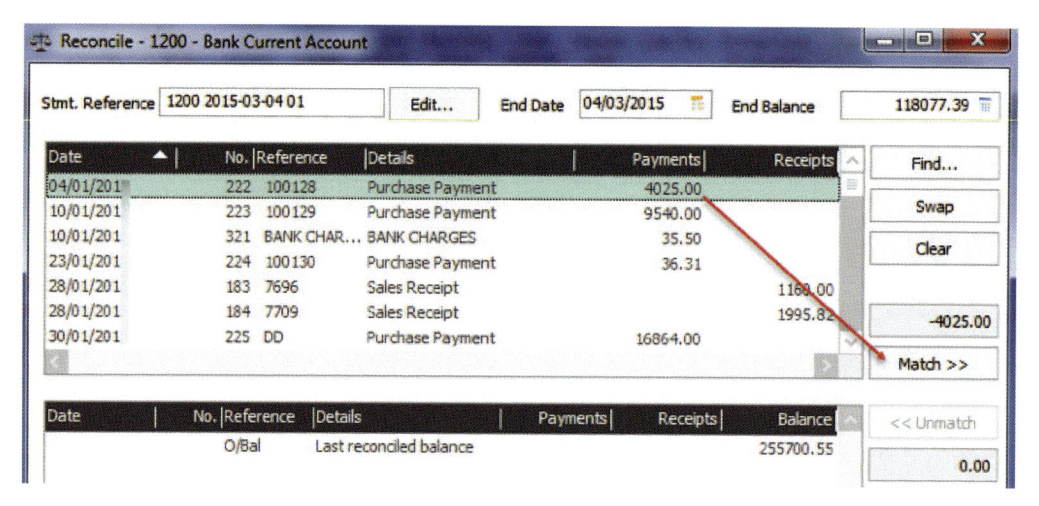

fig. 118

- *The item is removed from the top unmatched pane - section A, and appears in the lower Matched pane – section B as illustrated Fig. 119*

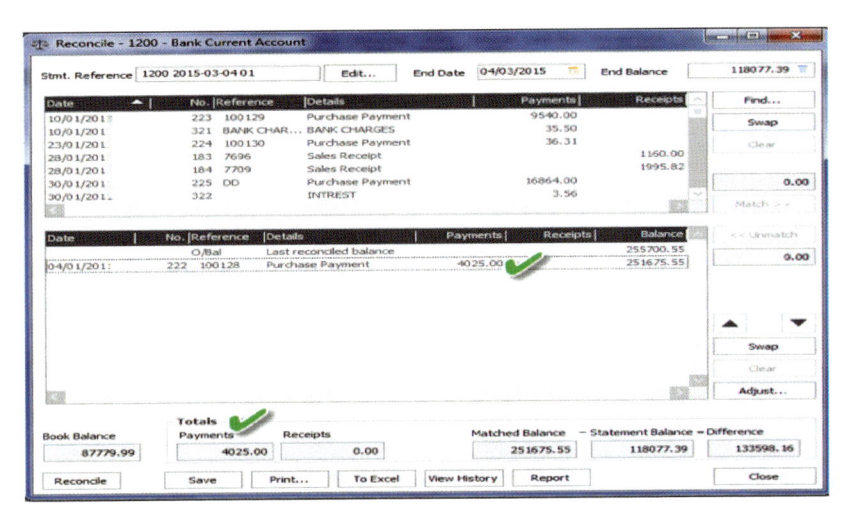

fig. 119

- As you move transactions from the top pane to the lower pane, the matched balance and difference values in the Totals section (see green ticks in the figure above) of the window change automatically.

- Transactions are positioned in the lower Matched against Statement pane – section B in the order in which they are moved into the area. Any transaction within this area that is associated with a negative bank balance appears red.

- To move a transaction from the lower Matched against Statement pane to the unmatched upper pane, single click on the transaction to highlight it, then click unmatch, as illustrated in the figure below.

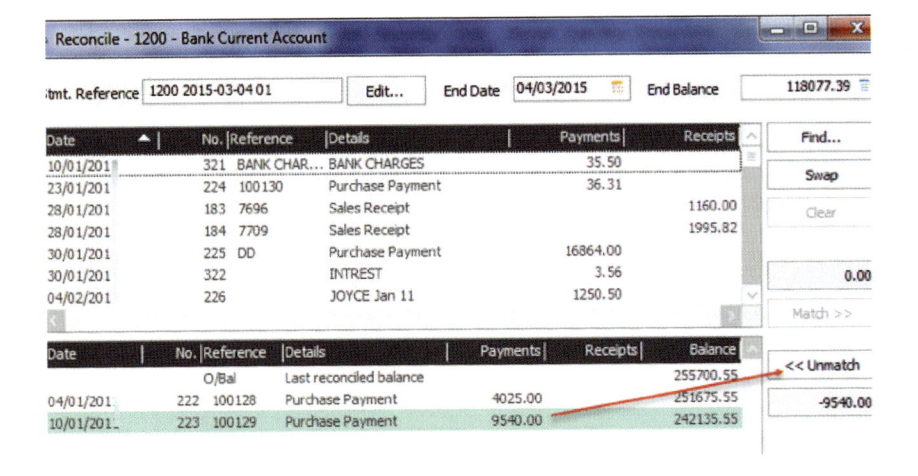

fig. 120

Once you become proficient in the reconciliation procedure, you can speed up the process by multi-selecting transactions to match / unmatch.

ii. Making adjustments during the reconciliation process

- To add a transaction to your bank records from the reconciliation window (for either payment or receipt), click Adjust and the Adjustment window opens. Select the adjustment type you want to make, then click OK to open the appropriate transaction entry window. Enter the adjustment details then click Save. The adjustment will be displayed in the Matched against Statement area of the window – section B.

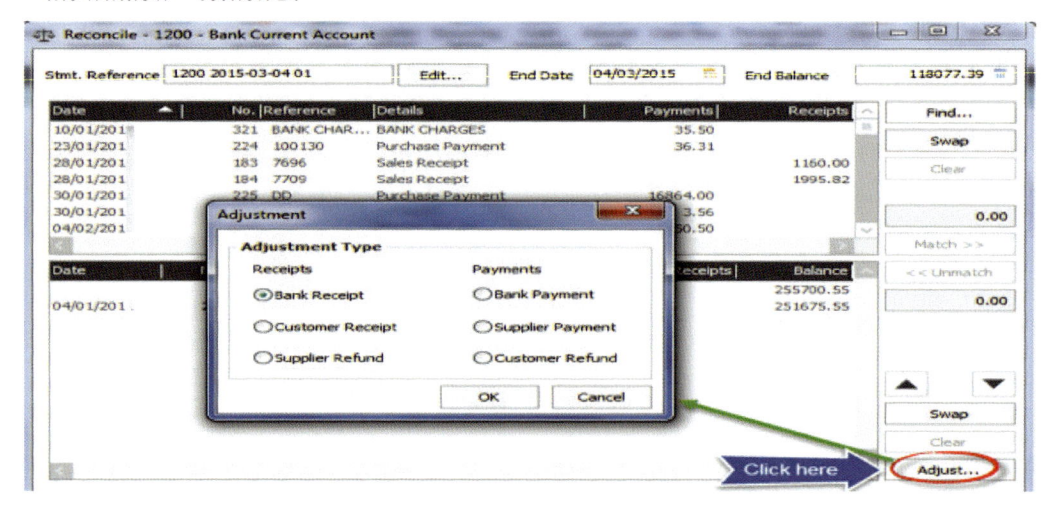

fig. 121

iii. Rearranging the order of transactions during reconciliations process

- To change the order of transactions in the matched against statement area – section B during a reconciliation process, select a transaction and then click the up and down arrows to reposition the transaction within the list as illustrated in Fig. 122.

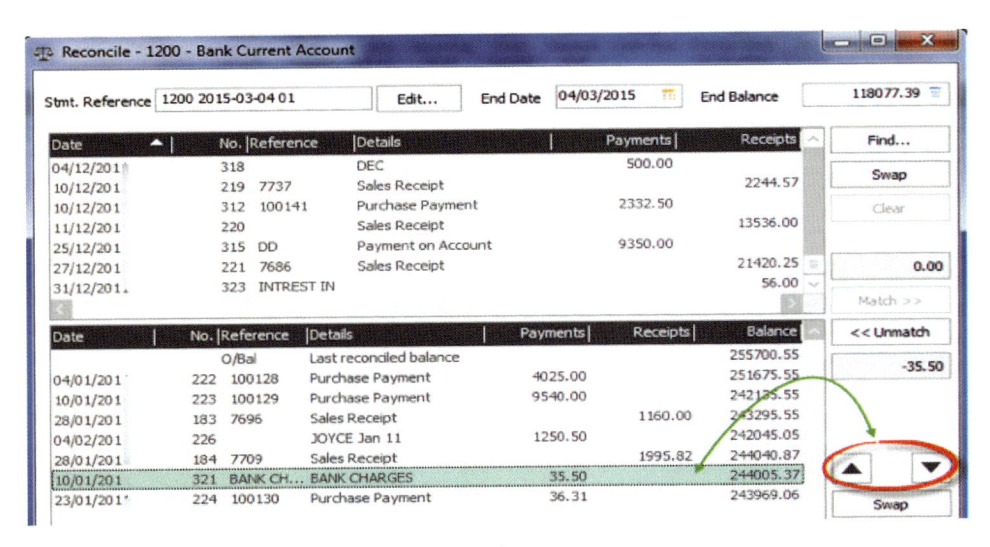

fig. 122

- Once you are satisfied you have completed the reconciliation, that is all transactions in the bank statement have been matched and; Statement Balance = Matched Balance with the difference being zero, click Reconcile (at the bottom left of the bank reconciliation window – see Fig. 123)

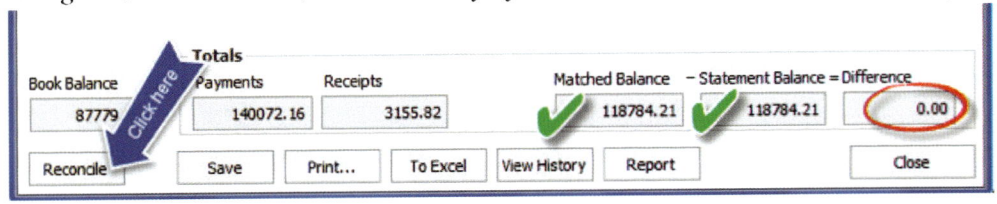

fig. 123

While the account is being reconciled a progress indicator is displayed. Once complete the Bank Reconciliation window closes.

If the statement balance and matched balances are not equal you can choose to:

- *Investigate and rectify the problem. Remember, you can put the bank reconciliation on hold and return to finish it later by clicking save (it is next to the reconcile button). Any transactions you add to your software to rectify the problem are made available for reconciliation, provided their date does not exceed the reconciliation's Statement (End) Date.*

To put the bank reconciliation on hold, click save, then OK when prompted to do so.

THE ACCOUNTS ASSISTANT JOB MANUAL

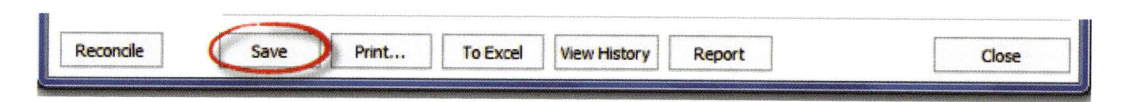

fig. 124

To get back to your bank reconciliation window after saving your work, click on bank accounts> then select the account you were reconciling (e.g. bank current account 1200) then click on the reconcile tab to open the reconciliation window of your saved work – see *Fig. 125*

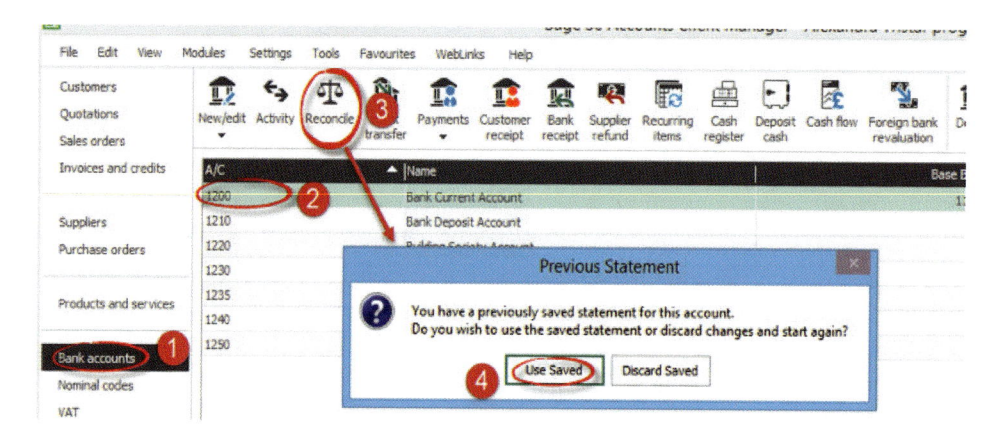

fig. 125

SECTION 6
DEBTOR MANAGEMENT

TASK 23

Collecting outstanding debts

Here, we are going to look at how to effectively collect outstanding debts from debtors and how to avoid bad debts occurring.

Here is how to do it:

    a) Produce the credit managers report from Sage 50 and use it to 'chase' for overdue account balances.

Follow the instructions as illustrated in the figure below (steps 1- 8). After step 8, you will see the credit managers report which you will need to double check its accuracy with source documents and make arrangements to do some debt collection if there are any which the credit managers report will highlight.

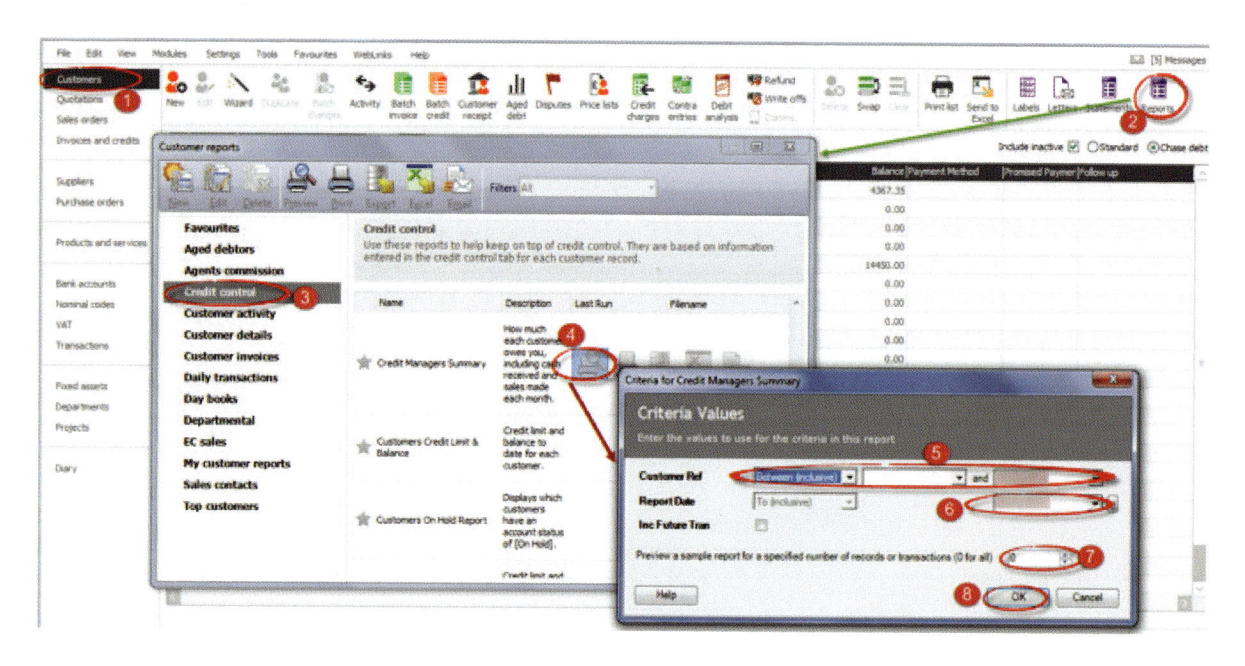

fig. 126

Steps as illustrated in the figure above:

1. Click on Customers
2. Then click on reports
3. Customer reports window will appear, Click on Credit control
4. Now scroll down and find credit managers summary report and click on the preview tab. Criteria for Credit Managers summary window will appear
5. Select the details in the customer ref as required
6. Select the report date as required or desired
7. Leave this number as zero
8. Click OK
9. Double check the accuracy of the report and print it out if it's okay.

Now, let's look at…

b) 12 steps to take to collect outstanding debts from debtors

i. Send the customer a current account statement or gentle reminder.

ii. 5 working days after sending the statement check to see whether the amount has been paid.

iii. If the amount has not been paid, telephone the client and discuss the reason for non-payment, remind them of their credit terms, and agree a payment date.

iv. Write a letter to the client summarising the telephone conversation and noting the agreed payment date.

v. Make a note on the system of the date payment should be received. Use communication tab on customer record window from Sage to make a note.

vi. If payment is not received by the agreed date telephone the client and remind them of your previous discussion.

vii. Agree a date for payment (or direct debit/credit card if applicable).

viii. Write a letter to the client summarising the telephone conversation and noting the agreed payment date.

ix. Make a note on the system of the date payment should be received.

x. If payment is not received by the agreed date telephone the client.

xi. Write a letter to the client summarising the telephone conversation and noting the date court proceedings will commence.

xii. Make a note on the system of the date payment should be received.

xiii. If payment is not received within the specified time then continue with the County Court procedure.

xiv. Make arrangements to attend court.

> **"So teach us to number our days, that we may apply our hearts unto wisdom"**
>
> –Psalm 90:12

SECTION 7

STOCK CONTROL

TASK 24

Doing stock take & posting opening and closing stock values

i. Doing stock take

For a variety of reasons, the stock you actually have in the physical count might be different to the level recorded in your sage 50 software.

To update the stock levels, you can use the stock take option to enter the correct quantities you currently have in stock.

When you enter the current stock levels for your products, an adjustment in or out is posted automatically in sage in your stock activity to correct the stock level.

Here is how to do it:

Click on products and services, then select the required product records or click swap to select all the products, then click on stock take. See illustration in the figure below.

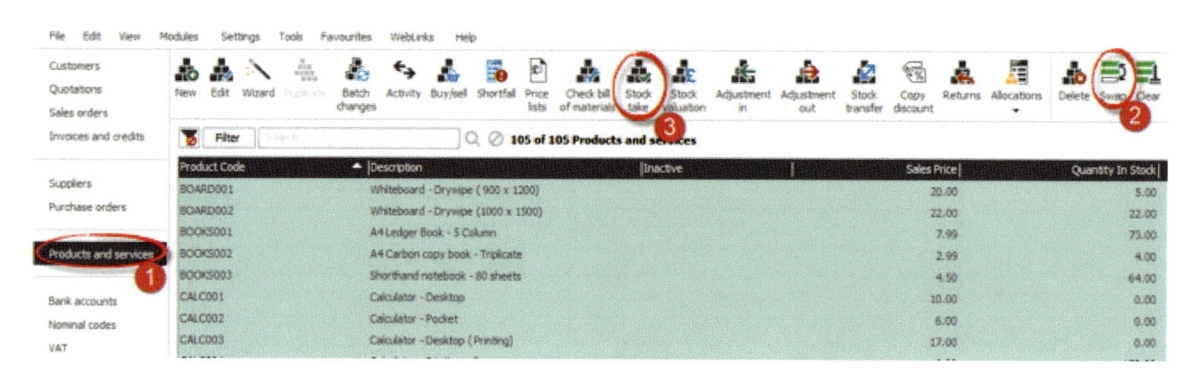

fig. 127

After step 3 in the figure above, a window similar to *Fig. 128* might appear if you have non

SECTION 7 - STOCK CONTROL

stock or service items selected. Click OK to continue.

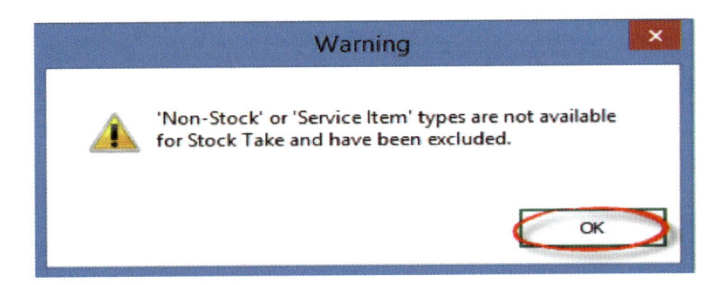

fig. 128

Once you click OK, a figure similar to the one below will appear.

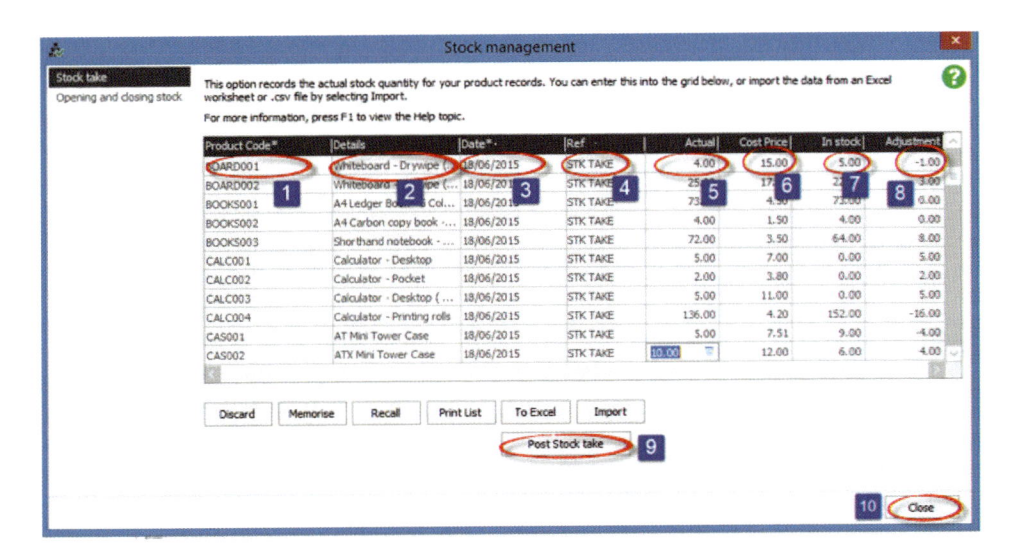

fig. 129

If you selected swap in the preceding section, the information in this window will be automatically populated for you with adjustments only needed in 3 and 5 in the figure above. Otherwise,

complete the Stock take as follows:

1. From the drop-down list, choose the required product code.

2. The product code description appears automatically.

3. Enter the date of the stock take.

103

4. *STK TAKE automatically appears here, however you can change this if required.*

5. *Enter the actual number of the selected product item you currently have in stock.*

Note: If you enter a value of zero, that indicates that you have nothing in stock and therefore an adjustment is posted to adjust the stock to 0.00. It is important to ensure that you do not enter a zero value or leave this field blank when you post your stock take details unless you actually have zero in stock.

6. *The cost price automatically appears here.*

7. *This is the current quantity in stock.*

8. *The adjustment value. This is the difference between the in stock and Actual figures.*

If you currently have more items in stock than was previously recorded, this appears as a positive value. If you have fewer items, the adjustment figure appears as a negative value.

9. *Don't forget to click Post Stock take, then*

10. *Click Close.*

ii. Posting opening and closing stock values

Why do we have to do this?

This is because it's really important to ensure that the profit figures are accurate. If you have unsold stock at the end of the month/period you need to include this in the profit figures to get an accurate cost of sales.

Your first opening stock value should be posted as part of your opening balances. You should then post opening and closing stock transactions each month/period to adjust the profit and loss calculation, so that the profit figure for a specific period takes into account any unsold stock.

By default, the Profit and Loss report calculates the Gross Profit as:

Gross Profit = Sales - Purchases

However, if you post opening and closing stock transactions the Profit and Loss report calculates the Gross Profit as:

Gross Profit = Sales - Cost of Sales*

*Cost of Sales = Opening Stock + Purchases - Closing Stock

(you remember this from your theoretical studies at college or university, don't you?)

Anyway, to post the opening and closing stock, here is what you need to do.

Click on Modules, then select Wizards from the drop down menu, then click on Opening and Closing stock. See illustration in the figure below.

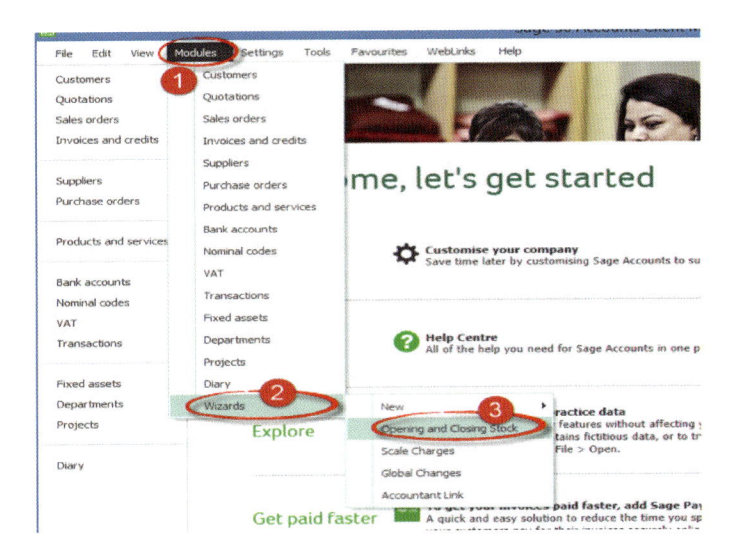

fig. 130

Once you click on opening and closing stock – step 3 in the figure above, a window similar to *Fig. 131* will appear;

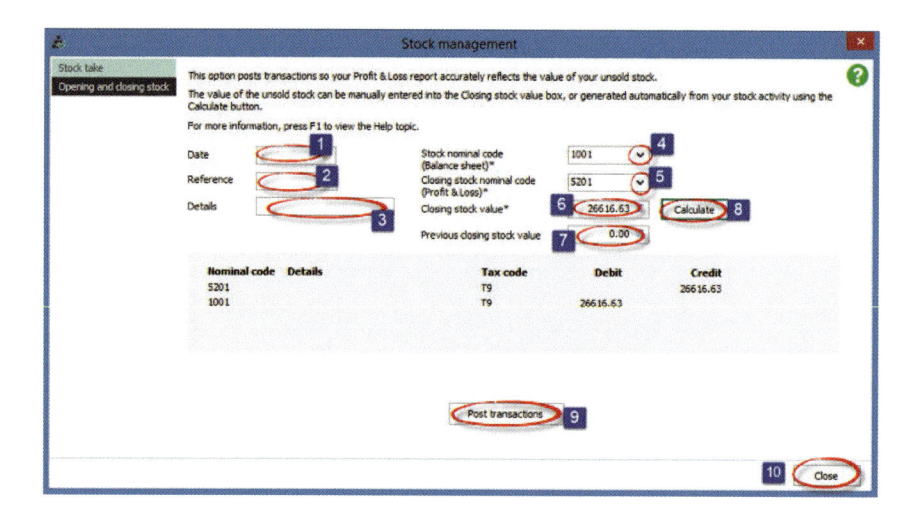

fig. 131

Complete the Opening and closing stock window as follows:

1. Type in here the date for the posting the opening and closing stock values

2. Enter a reference for the transaction. You can make up your own reference

3. Enter the details, for example May closing stock

4. From the drop-down list, choose the required nominal code. By default, this is 1001.

5. From the drop-down list, choose the required nominal code. By default, this is 5201.

6. Enter the closing stock value.

7. Enter the previous closing stock value, this is also your opening stock value for the period.

8. Alternatively, to automatically calculate closing stock value, click Calculate.

The Calculate button generates the figure by multiplying the quantity in stock by the average cost price for every product. In Sage 50 Accounts plus and Sage 50 Accounts Professional, you can check this by running the Product Valuation by Stock Category report. This report is not available in Sage 50 Accounts, Sage Instant Accounts and Sage Instant Plus.

Note: This valuation is not date specific and is based on all stock transactions that have been posted to date. If required, you can change this value.

9. Check the transactions to ensure the details are correct then click Post transactions to complete the process, then

10. Click Close.

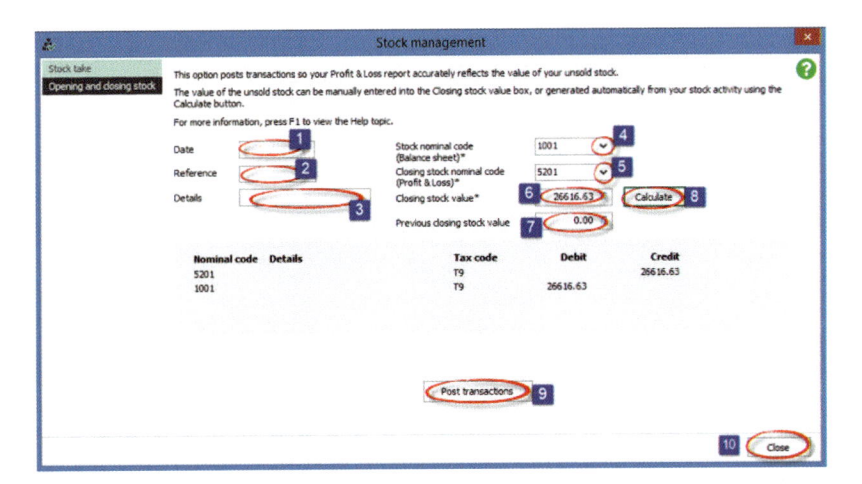

fig. 132

"To make no mistakes is not in the power of man; but from their errors and mistakes, the wise and good learn wisdom for the future"

–*Plutarch (46 AD - 120 AD)*

SECTION 8
NOMINAL ERROR CHECK & CORRECTIONS

TASK 25

Checking nominal ledger balances & correcting errors

Let's look at an example of how to correct an error discovered in a ledger account. The figure below is an example of a trial balance from Sage 50 accounts software. We are particularly going to check the accuracy of the balance of the nominal account 7502 (office stationery).

```
Date:                                    Tristar progress ltd -                      Page:    1
Time:   22:18:15                          Period Trial Balance

To Period:     Month 12, December 2015

N/C        Name                                          Debit              Credit
0020       Plant and Machinery                       32,125.89
0030       Office Equipment                          17,971.06
0040       Furniture and Fixtures                       495.32
1100       Debtors Control Account                  58,761.46
1235       Cash Register                             4,380.00
2100       Creditors Control Account                                     192,898.51
2200       Sales Tax Control Account                                       4,393.71
2201       Purchase Tax Control Account             10,328.50
4000       Sales Type A                                                   36,562.35
4001       Sales Type B                                                   22,185.40
5000       Materials Purchased                     121,801.38
5001       Materials Imported                        1,012.50
7100       Rent                                      3,846.81
7102       Water Rates                               1,774.27
7103       General Rates                             1,380.00
7200       Electricity                                 498.38
7201       Gas                                         122.50
7300       Vehicle Fuel                                 51.06
7304       Miscellaneous Motor Expenses                919.15
7502       Office Stationery                           165.31
7601       Audit Fees                                  300.00
7801       Cleaning                                    106.38
                                       Totals:    256,039.97             256,039.97
```

fig. 133

- To check the integrity of the balance of the nominal account 7502; click on Nominal codes, then click on activity then type 7502 on the nominal code section and press enter as illustrated in Fig. 134.

SECTION 8 - NOMINAL ERROR CHECK & CORRECTIONS

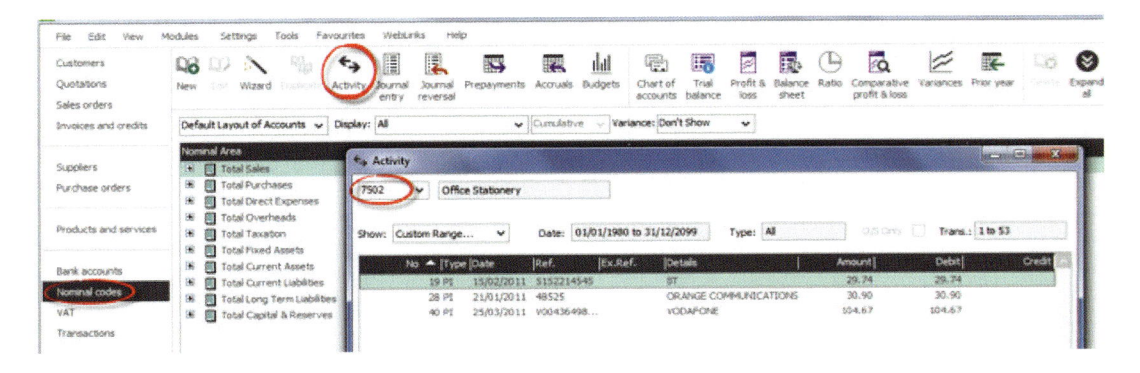

fig. 134

- *Now check the transactions under the nominal account 7502 to make sure that they relate to office stationery as 7502 is the nominal account code for office stationery.*

Should you find any transaction(s) that is/are not related to office stationery listed under this code in this case, you will have to move it to the right nominal account.

Here is how to do it:

- *Let's pick up from the last step in the figure above; remember we clicked on nominal codes>activity>then typed 7502 and a window similar to the one below appeared.*

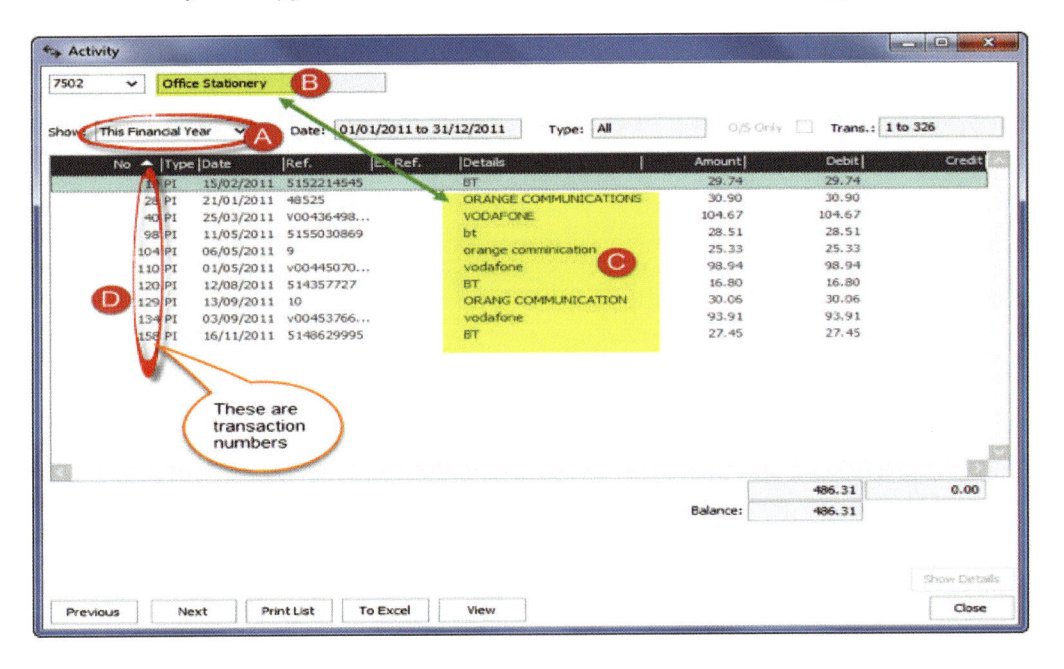

fig. 135

111

A. Choose the period you want to view from the drop down

B. The description in B should be related to the details in C and as you can see from the figure above, office stationery (B) has no bearing to telephones as the details in C suggest.

In this case therefore, all the transactions (D) need to be moved away from office stationery account (7502).

Let's suppose you are now going to move transaction 40 shown in the figure above; the first thing you will have to do is note the transaction number (in this case 40), then click transactions – see below.

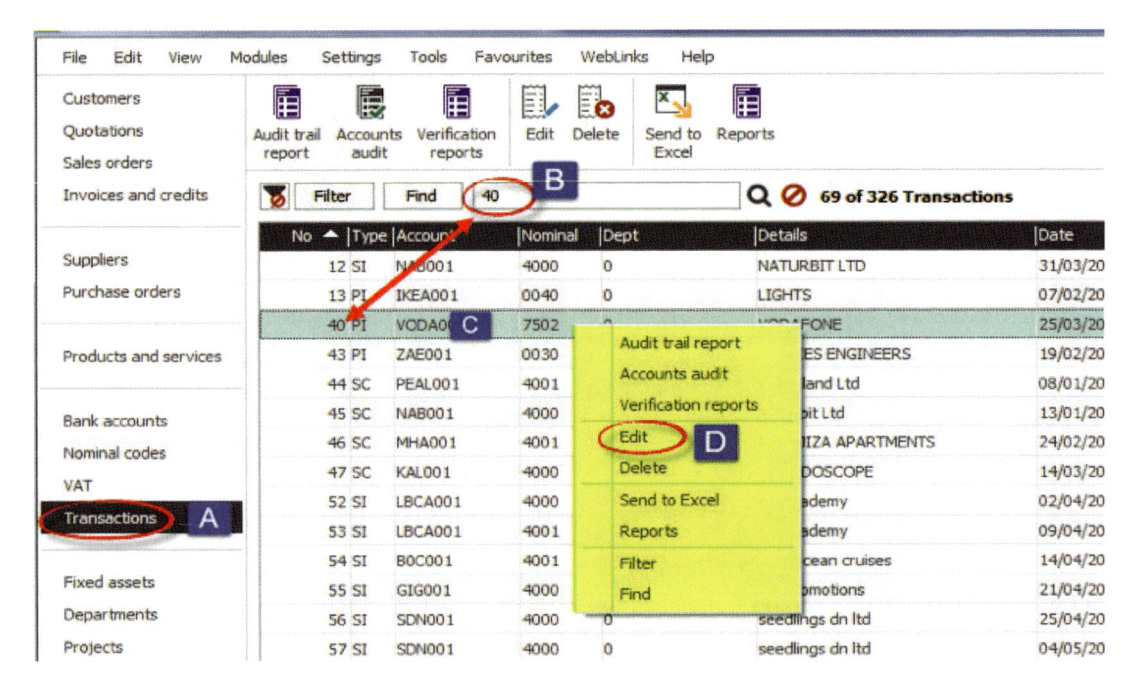

fig. 136 A. Click on transactions

B. Type in the transaction number you want to edit (in this case - transaction 40) on to the search box

and press enter on your computer key board

C. Now locate the transaction from the search results that appear and right click on it. The yellow shaded window will appear (the actual window is not actually yellow, it is shaded yellow here for illustrative purposes)

D. Select edit and the window similar to Fig. 137 will appear

SECTION 8 - NOMINAL ERROR CHECK & CORRECTIONS

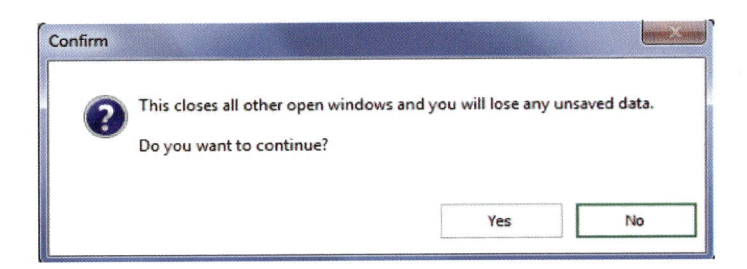

fig. 137

E. Click yes to continue.

When you click yes, a window similar to the one below will appear.

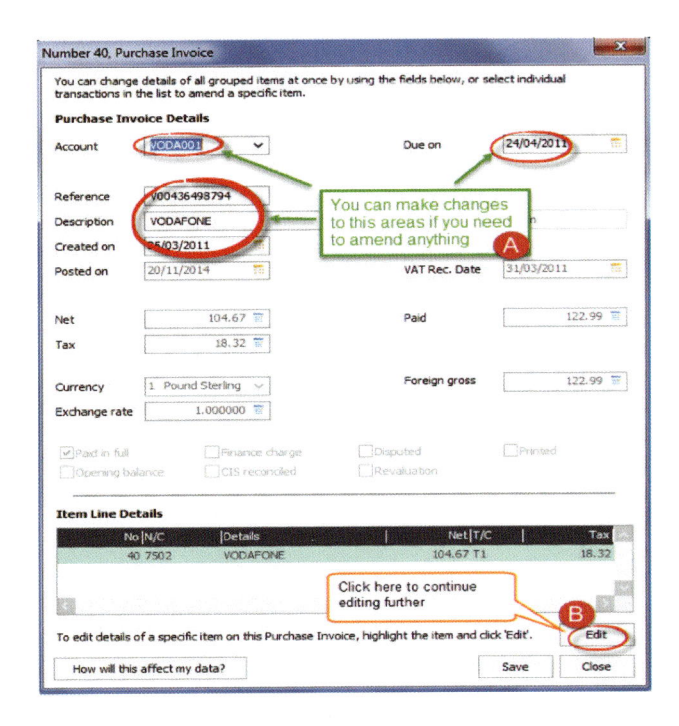

fig. 138

A. If you want to amend the account, the due date of the invoice, invoice reference, description on the invoice or the date the invoice was created, you can do it here. Otherwise

B. If you want to make further edits like changing the nominal codes and amounts(figures) in the invoice then click edit at the bottom right of the window as illustrated in B in the figure above. Once you click edit, a figure similar to Fig. 139 will appear

113

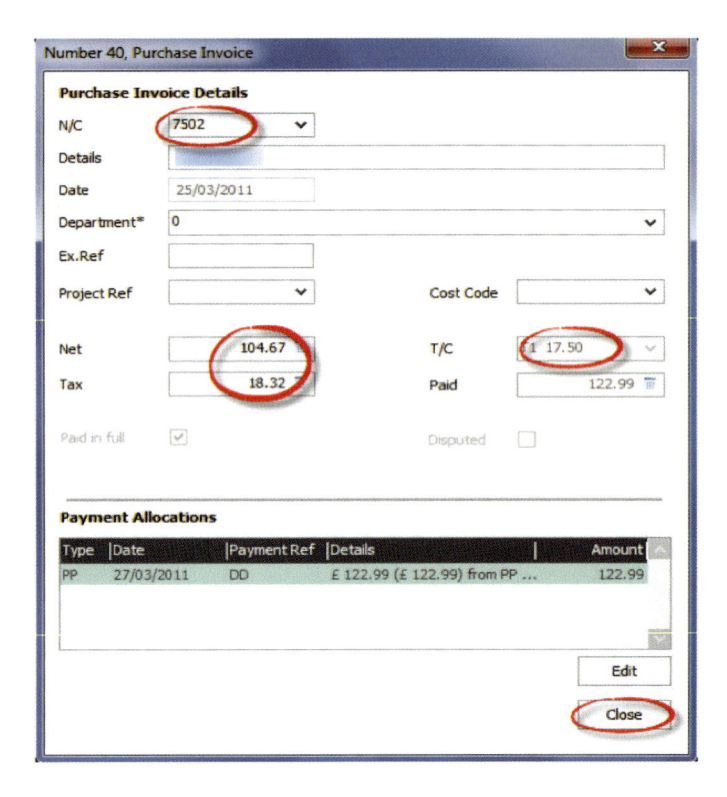

fig. 139

- *Make any further necessary changes like changing the nominal code, the net amount or VAT including the tax code used and remember to click close, then click save.*

A window will popup asking you this: "Do you want to post this changes?"

Click yes.

That's it, you have now successfully made the necessary changes.

SECTION 9
PRODUCING ACCOUNTING REPORTS

TASK 26

Producing common accounting reports:

We will now produce some of the common reports that you might be asked to produce during the course of your work. Here they are:

- *Trial balance report:*
- *Purchase day book(supplier invoices)*
- *Sales ledger activity report*
- *Bank reconciliation report*
- *Transactions audit trail report*
- *Profit & Loss management report*

i. Trial balance

- *Click on Nominal codes > then click on Trial balance as illustrated in the figure below*

fig. 140

- *The window similar to one below will appear, choose whether you want to print the trial balance right away or preview it or save it to file or email it, then click Run as illustrated in Fig. 141.*

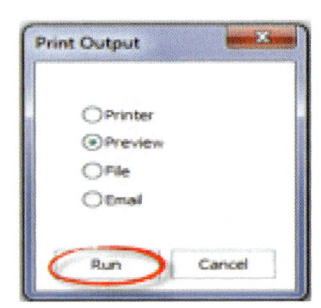

If you select the file option on the print output window, the window similar to the one below will appear, all you will have to do then is to select the location to save the file, file name and file type (see 1, 2, 3 and 4 in the figure below)

fig. 141

SECTION 9 PRODUCING ACCOUNTING REPORTS

fig. 142

- If you choose: printer, preview and email options on the print output window as shown in the figure above, a window similar to the figure below will appear.

Click on the drop down arrow as shown in *Fig. 143* to select the period you want the report for, e.g. month 12: December 2015.

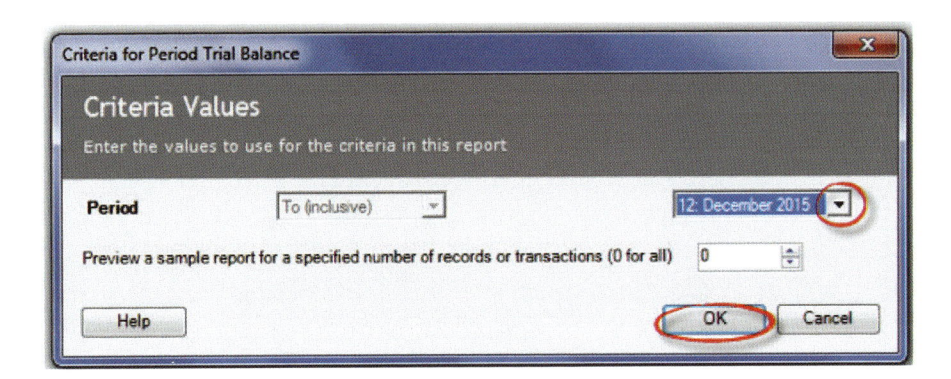

fig. 143

- Once you select the period, click Ok and you will see the preview of the trial balance and you should be able to print it or attach it to your email ready to be sent.

- You will need to check the balance on each nominal ledger account in the trial balance to make sure that the reported balance is accurate. In essence you have to check that the ledger balances are free from errors of principle, transposition errors, errors of commission etc.

117

ii. Purchases day book (supplier invoices) report

Follow the steps as illustrated in the diagram below to produce this report in Sage:

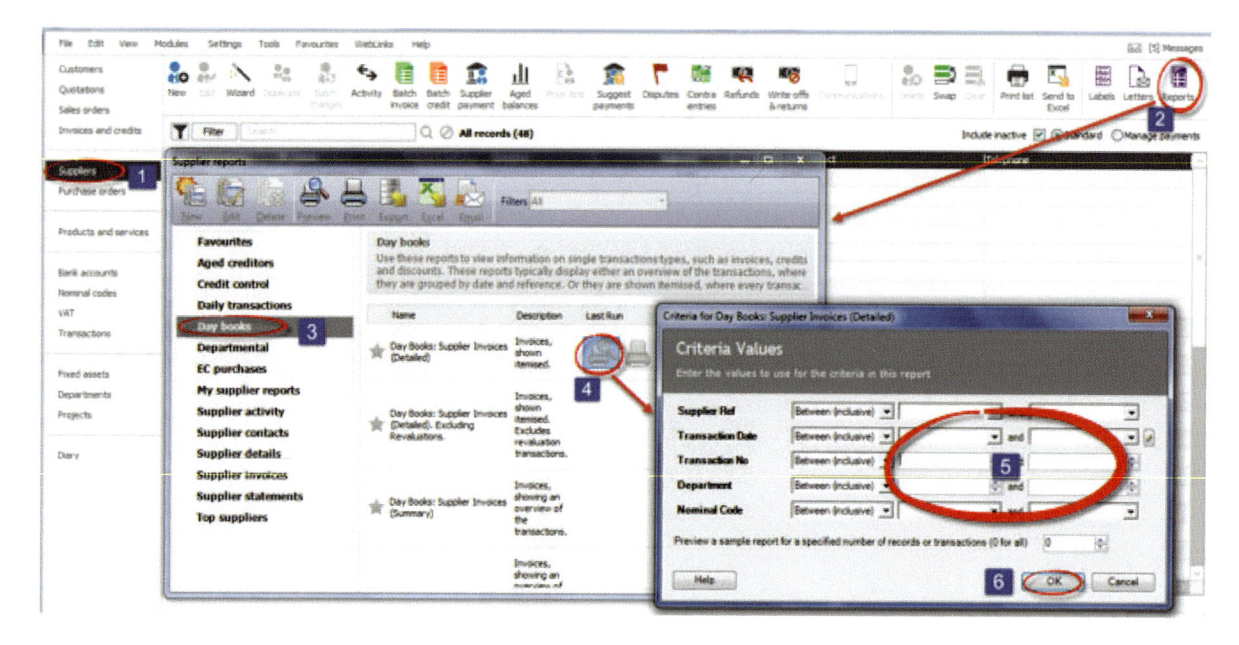

fig. 144

Here is how to do it:

1. Click on Suppliers

2. Then click on reports at the top right hand corner of the Sage program. The supplier reports window will appear

3. Click on Day books at the left section of the supplier's reports window.

4. Day books reports will appear at the right hand side of the supplier's reports window. Scroll down and find Day Books: Supplier invoices (detailed) report and click on the preview tab.

The criteria for Day Books: Supplier invoices (Detailed) window will appear

5. Fill out this section as required or necessary: the supplier reference range, department range transaction date range, transaction number range and nominal code range.

6. Don't forget to click OK to preview the report

iii. Sales ledger accounts (customer accounts), showing all transactions within the account

Follow the sequence of numbered steps in the figure below from your Sage 50 accounts software.

fig. 145

Here is how to do it:

1. Click on Customers

2. Then click on reports at the top right hand corner of the Sage program. The Customer reports window will appear

3. Click on Customer activity at the left section of the customer's reports window.

Customer Activity section will appear at the right hand side of the customer's reports window.

4. Find Customer Activity (Detailed) report and click on the preview tab.

The criteria for Customer Activity (Detailed) window will appear

5. Fill out this section as required or necessary: the customer reference range, transaction date range, transaction number range, department range and nominal code range.

6. If you want to include brought forward transactions and exclude later payments, tick this check boxes

7. Leave the number here as zero if you want to view all records of transactions within the accounts

8. Don't forget to click OK to preview the report

iv. Reconciled bank transaction report for the period

From your sage 50 accounts software, after clicking on bank accounts –step 1 in the figure below, select the account you want the report for e.g. a/c 1200 then follow the inset steps (1-8) as illustrated in the figure below to produce your bank reconciliation report.

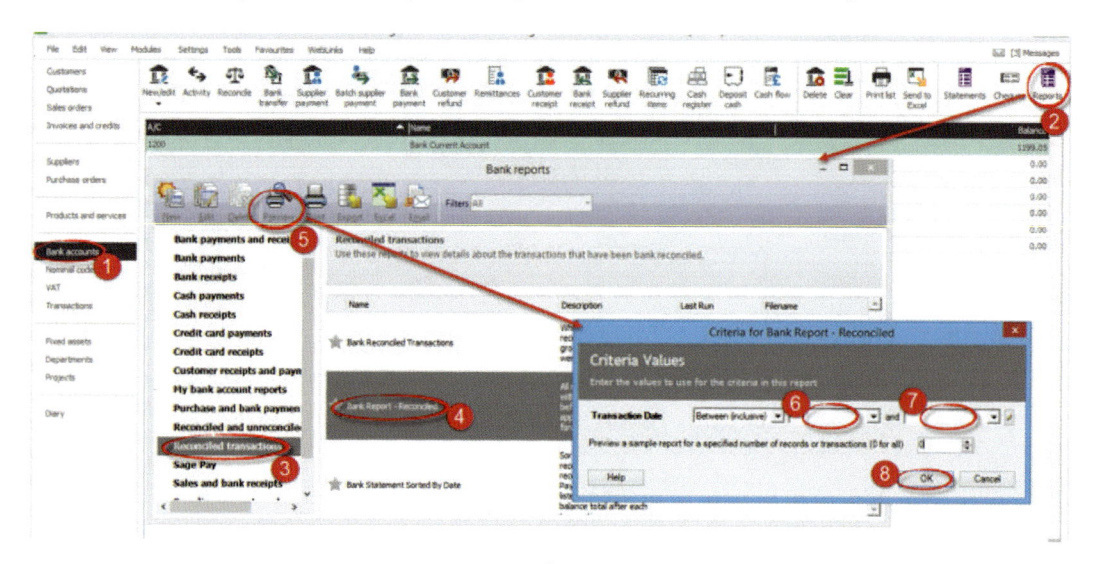

fig. 146

Here how to do it:

1. Click on Bank accounts

2. Then click on reports at the top right hand corner of the Sage program. The Bank current account reports window will appear

3. Click on Reconciled transactions at the left section of the Bank current account reports window.

    Reconciled transactions section will appear at the right hand side of the Bank current account reports window.

4. Find Bank Report – Reconciled transaction report, and

5. Click on the preview tab.

The criteria for Bank Report - Reconciled window will appear

6. Fill out this section as required or necessary: the transaction date range – start date and

7. Transaction date range – end date.

8. Don't forget to click OK to preview the report

v. Audit trail report

This report shows all, transactions entered into sage. It includes even deleted and cancelled or amendments made. Literally, it contains everything posted into the ledgers in Sage 50 Accounts within the financial year.

Here are the steps to follow to produce the audit trail report showing all transactions within the ledgers:

1. Click on transactions, then > click on audit trail as shown below

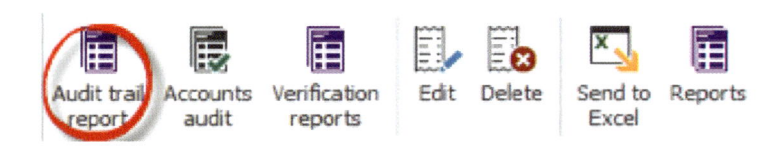

fig. 147

2. After you click on audit trail report, the audit trail report generator window similar to the one below will appear.

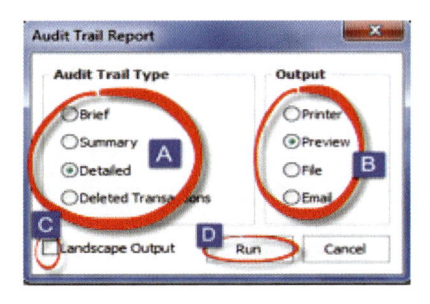

fig. 148

A. Select the Audit trail report type required: Brief, Summary. Detailed or Deleted transactions

B. Select the report output path. You have options of printer, preview, file and email. Printer option will send the reports selected in B to the printer, preview option will display the reports selected in B *above on your computer screen, file option will open a window for you to select the destination where you want to save the reports and email option will open your default email sending account (if configured) and attach the reports ready for you to send to your recipient.*

C. *Select this check box if you want the report in a landscape view*

D. *Don't forget to click Run after step B & C*

vi. Profit and loss management account report.

This report is a detailed profit and loss account showing month by month totals of the profit and loss account.

Here is how to get this report. Follow the steps as illustrated in *Fig. 149*:

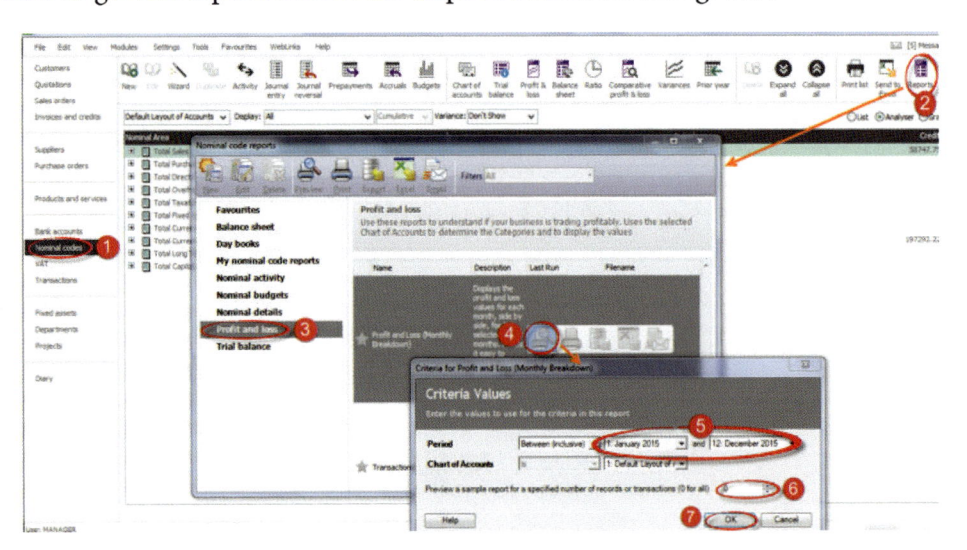

fig. 149

Do the following:

1. Click on Nominal codes

2. Then click on reports at the top right hand corner of the Sage program. The Nominal code reports window will appear

3. Click on Profit & loss at the left section of the Nominal code reports window.

Profit & loss section will appear at the right hand side of the Nominal codes window.

4. Scroll down and find profit & loss (monthly breakdown) report and click on the preview tab.

The criteria for profit & loss (monthly breakdown) window will appear

5. Fill out this section as required or necessary: Period (this should be for the month range required for the report e.g. January to December, June to December, March to September etc.

6. Leave the number in here as zero if you want to view all records of transactions within the profit and loss report

7. Don't forget to click OK to preview the report

> **"It is your duty to protect what belongs to you, ignore to do so at your own peril"**
>
> *–Sterling Libs*

SECTION 10

DATA SECURITY

TASK 27

Ensuring safety & security of accounting data

Using passwords is a very essential part of data security and as such it is important that you protect your logon with a password.

If you want to change your password, here is how to do it:

- *Click on settings, then click on change password - see below*

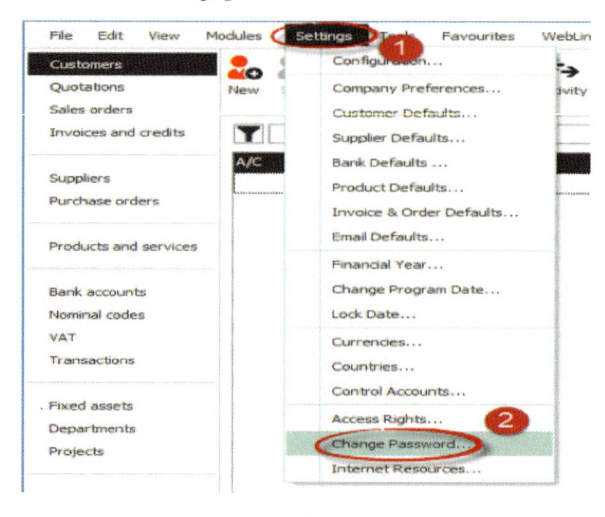

fig. 150

Once you click change password as illustrated above – step 2, you will see a dialogue box similar to *Fig. 151*

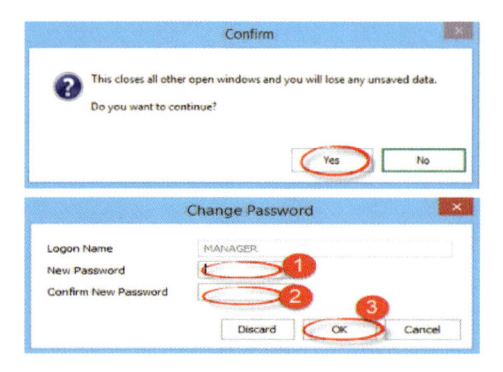

Click yes to continue and you will see a change password window similar to the one below
Follow the inset steps (1-3) to change the password

fig. 151

SECTION 10 - DATA SECURITY

TASK 28

Backing up & restoring your work

Backing up accounting data

Here is what to do to back up your work:

Click on file and select back up – see *Fig. 152*

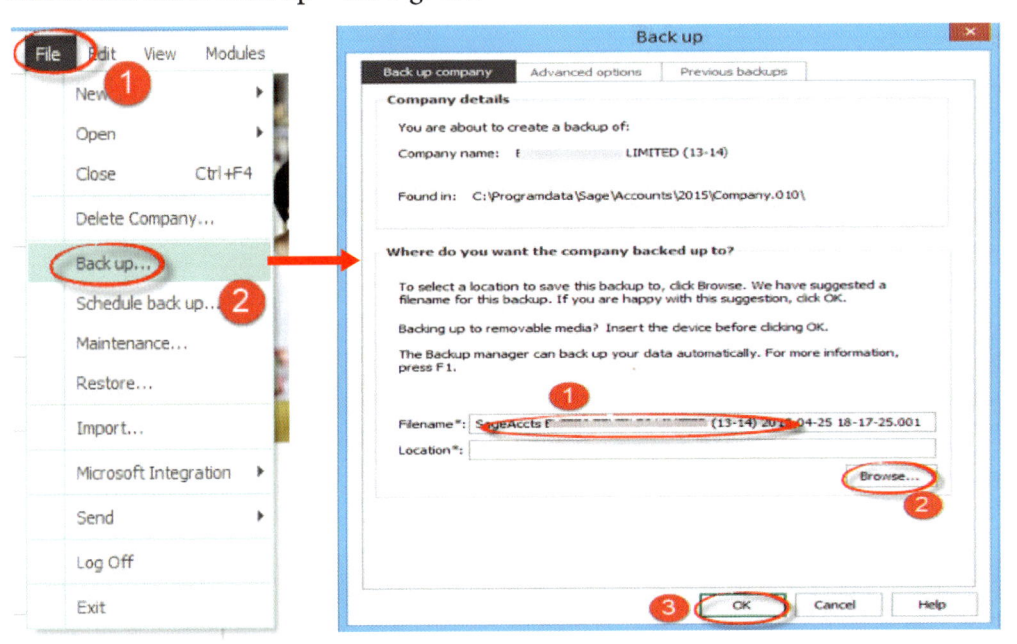

fig. 152

If after backing up your data you decide to close the Sage 50 program, a dialogue box (Exit program) will appear. There will be a message asking whether you would like to back up your data. Click No since you have already backed up your data.

Now, let's look at how to restore your back up later on to a different computer with Sage 50 accounts installed.

Restoring your back up

Here is a scenario;

Say for example after 3 days you come to work but are now using a different computer to the one you used previously. What would you do?

Well, as for long as the new computer has Sage 50 accounts installed on it, you can continue with your work by restoring your back up. Please note that the new computer must have a similar version to the one your backed up data is in or a higher version but never a lower version.

Right, let's now restore the back up.

Steps to take:

1. Start your computer up, then

2. Double click on the Sage 50 Accounts on your desktop

After you double click on the Sage icon on your desktop, a Select company window similar to the one below will appear.

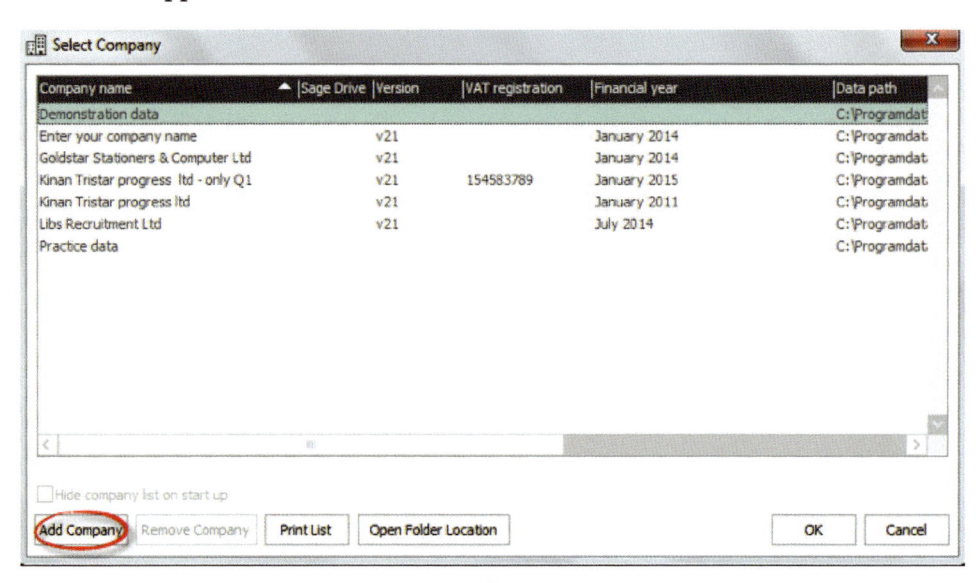

fig. 153

Click on add company – as shown in the figure above and an active set setup window similar to the one below will appear.

Select restore data from backup file and click browse (steps 1 & 2 in Fig. 154).

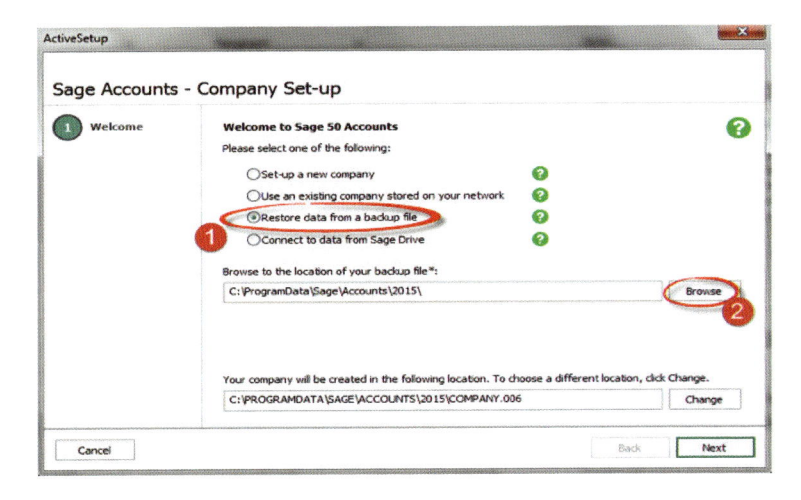

fig. 154

Once you click browse, you will see a window for use to select where your backed up data is

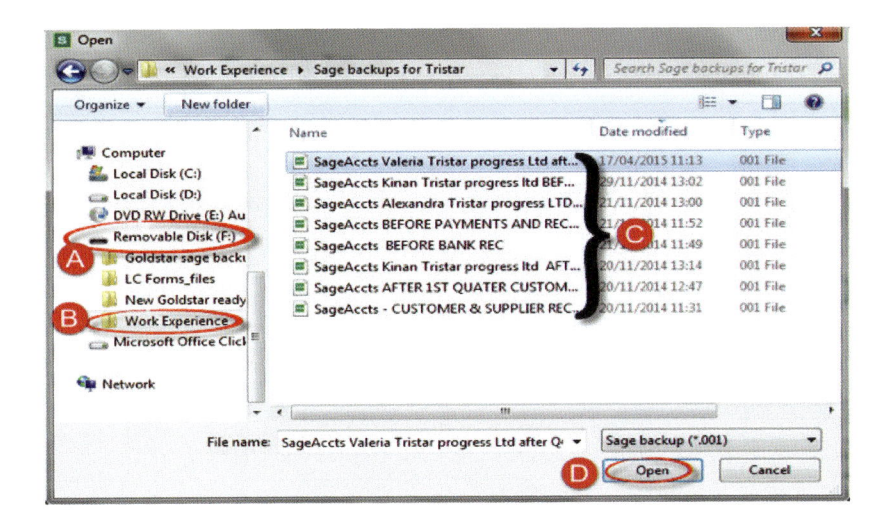

fig. 155

A. Locate your external drive (in this case removable disk F)

B. Locate the folder where you backed up your data if applicable

C. Select the latest backup from the list of your back up files

D. Click open to start restoring it to Sage 50 accounts – see Fig. 156

THE ACCOUNTS ASSISTANT JOB MANUAL

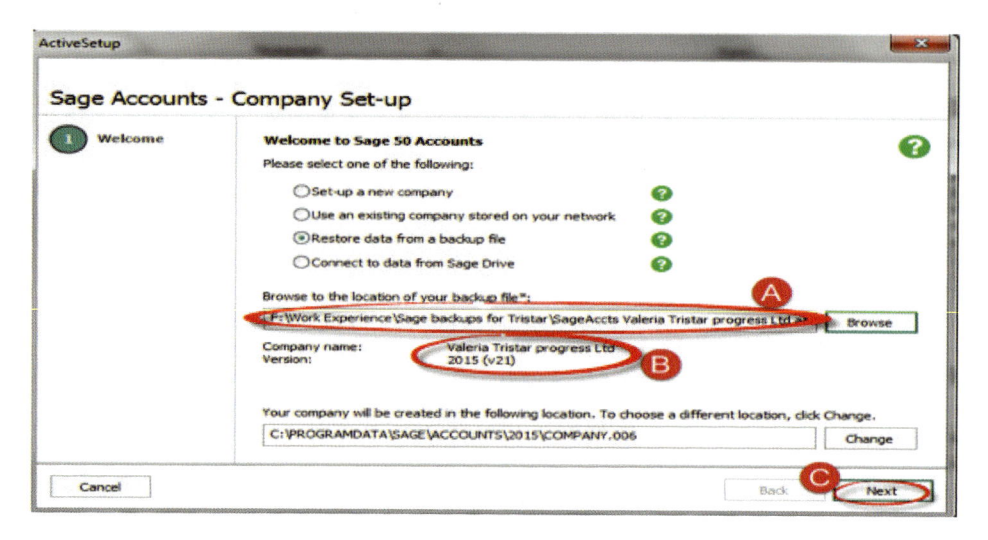

fig. 156

A. This shows your backed up data file now ready to be restored to Sage 50 accounts

B. This shows the name of the company (the backed up data company to be restored) and its financial year and the version number for Sage 50 it was backed in (in this version 21)

C. Click next to continue and restore the company.

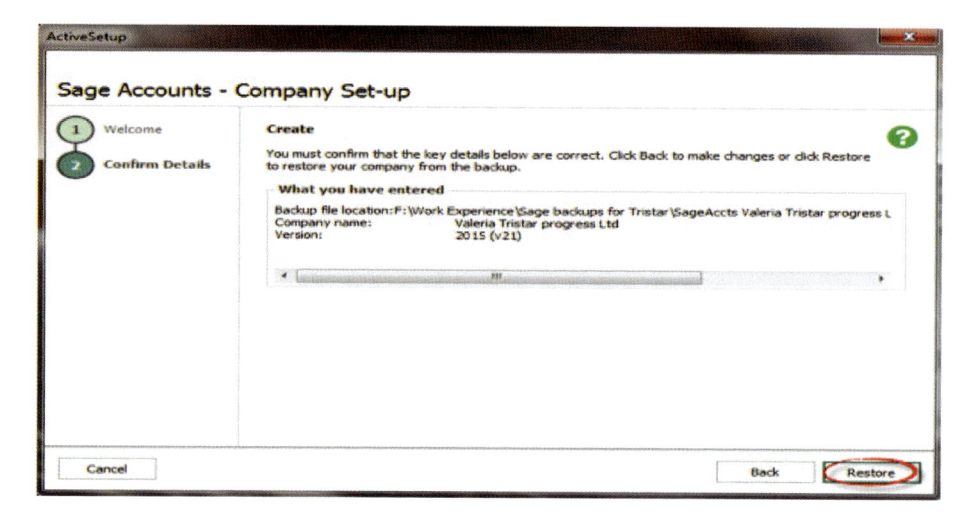

fig. 157

Confirm the details of the company to be restored and click restore as shown in the figure above.

Once you click restore, you will see – creating new company progress bar – see *Fig. 158*

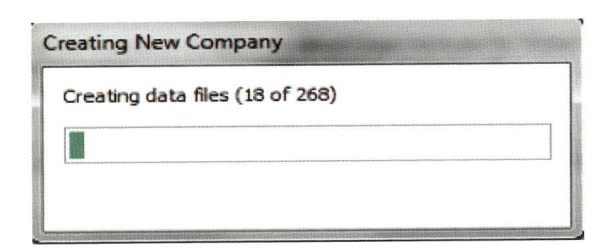

fig. 158

Once the company is restored on to Sage 50 accounts software, you will see a logon window requiring you to type in the logon details – see Fig. 159 below.

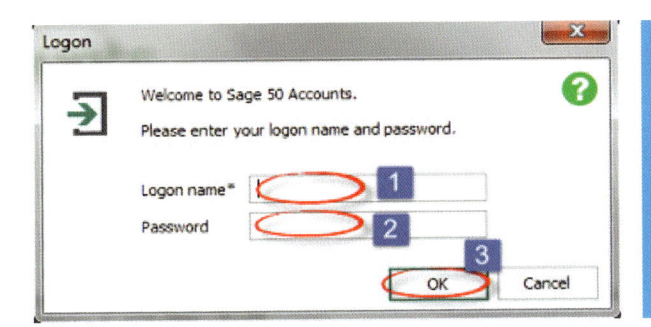

1. Type in here your logon name
2. Type in here your password if you have one or created one during the setup of the company
3. Click OK to complete log in

fig. 159

Once you have entered the correct logon details and clicked OK to login, you will be logged in to Sage and you will see a window similar to Fig. 160 below.

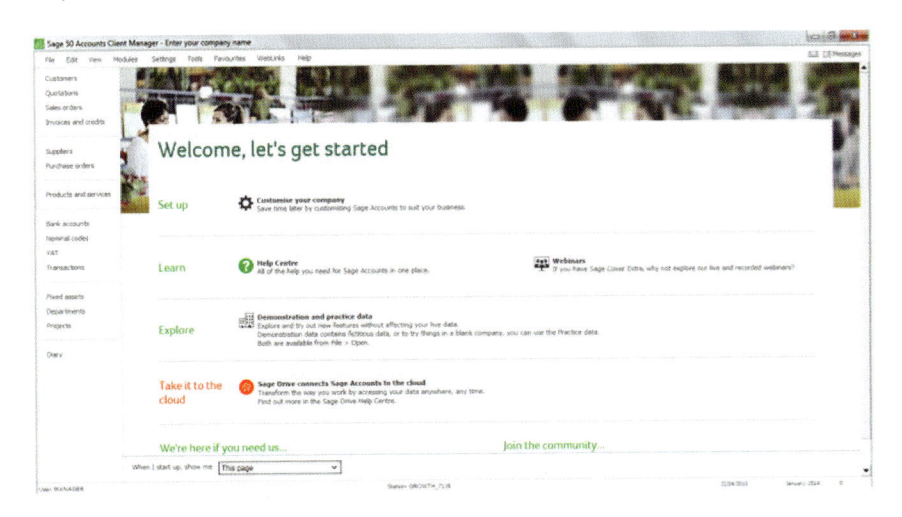

fig. 160

You can then change program date – See task 1.

131

THE ACCOUNTS ASSISTANT JOB MANUAL

═ TASK 29 ═

Checking your last processed transaction after restoring your data

To check where you last ended in your work click on transactions – see Fig. 161 below.

fig. 161

To check what the last transaction you processed was, follow the following steps as illustrated in the figure above:

1. Click on transactions

2. Click on the No. column heading such that the white arrow points up. This arranges the transaction numbers from the smallest to the biggest from top to bottom

3. Scroll down to the last transaction number, and there you have it, the last transaction number will tell you the details of the last transaction you posted.

In the figure above the last transaction is 178 and it is a sales payment (SP) received on account 1200 on the 08/12 from a customer with account code CDE001.

SECTION 11
ACCOUNTING ADMINISTRATION DUTIES

TASK 30

Administrative duties you might be required to do

Here are some common administrative duties that you will from time to time be involved in doing.

1. Sorting incoming post

Objective: To make sure that incoming mail is dealt with in a secure and controlled way.

    a. When mail is received, open envelopes addressed to the company

    b. Envelopes addressed to individual people within the company and marked as 'private and confidential' should be passed to them.

    c. Once mail is opened it should be date stamped, and distributed to the relevant people.

    d. If a courier arrives with a parcel, it should be checked for obvious damages and signed for.

    e. The parcel should then be passed onto the relevant person.

    f. If it is not addressed to anyone specific it should be opened and the contents checked to the delivery note attached to the parcel

    h. If the contents do not agree to the delivery note or are damaged in any way, contact the sender and advise them.

    i. If the contents are as stated on the delivery note, the goods should be distributed, and the delivery note passed to the Financial Accountant.

2. Sorting out outgoing post

Objective: To make sure that outgoing mail is dealt with in a secure and controlled way.

   a. All outgoing mail should be put in envelopes and any enclosures checked to ensure that they are included.

   b. Relevant information, such as PRIVATE AND CONFIDENTIAL, should be written clearly on the envelope.

   c. The correct postage should be applied. Make sure that you have an up to date postage rate list.

   d. All parcels should clearly show the receiver on the front and the sender (our company) on the back.

   e. If you need to send a parcel by courier ensure that the contents are securely wrapped.

   f. Make sure that you know the value of the contents of the parcel and its approximate weight.

   g. Contact the courier company and ask them to collect the parcel. Ask them for the cost of the service.

   h. You will need to give the value and weight so that they can calculate the cost of the delivery.

   i. Complete a purchase order form with the courier, parcel details and cost, and give this to the Financial Accountant.

3. Answering the telephone

Objective: To ensure that all telephone answering is done in a consistent way, to always delight the customer

   a. Ensure that someone is available to answer the telephone at all times.

   b. Keep a telephone message pad beside every telephone for taking messages.

   c. Always keep an up to date list of people who are out of the office, in meetings or not taking calls.

   d. When answering the telephone smile before you answer and use the script agreed by the team members.

   e. Don't interrogate the caller, and if the person that they would like to speak to is unavailable, then see if you can help.

   f. If a call needs returning, remind the person returning the call to make sure that it is returned.

4. Collecting outstanding debts

Here is how to collect outstanding debts from debtors – part of credit control

    xv. Send customer a current account statement or gentle reminder

    xvi. 5 working days after sending the statement check to see whether the amount has been paid.

    xvii. If the amount has not been paid, telephone the client and discuss the reason for non-payment, remind them of their credit terms, and agree a payment date.

    xviii. Write a letter to the client summarising the telephone conversation and noting the agreed payment date.

    xix. Make a note on the system of the date payment should be received.

    xx. If payment is not received by the agreed date telephone the client and remind them of your previous discussion.

    xxi. Agree a date for payment (or direct debit/credit card if applicable).

    xxii. Write a letter to the client summarising the telephone conversation and noting the agreed payment date.

    xxiii. Make a note on the system of the date payment should be received.

    xxiv. If payment is not received by the agreed date telephone the client.

    xxv. Write a letter to the client summarising the telephone conversation and noting the date court proceedings will commence.

    xxvi. Make a note on the system of the date payment should be received.

    xxvii. If payment is not received within the specified time then continue with the County Court procedure.

    xxviii. Make arrangements to attend court.

AFTERWORD

I believe accounting is a noble profession. Accountants support businesses in all industries in the economy and help facilitate business growth and economic development. If you desire a future of constant growth and change, accounting will certainly provide that for you.

We learn from our mistakes and hopefully, through this book your mistakes will be small ones as you make progress in your accounting profession.

Use the information in this book to learn the right way of doing accounts assistant regular day to day tasks. I trust this will be a stepping stone to your dreams in the accounting profession.

I like this quote by Walt Disney: "All our dreams can come true - if we have the courage to pursue them."

Thanks for giving me the opportunity to show you how to do the common tasks found in the job description of a bookkeeper, accounts assistant, sales & purchase ledger clerks. I hope you found the illustrations in this book useful. If you have any comments or feedback for me, drop me an email at books@sterlinglibs.com

Sterling Libs

STERLING LIBS
CHARTERED ACCOUNTANT

QUICK ORDER FORM

Postal Orders
Sterling Libs Books,
Level 33, 25 Canada Square,
Canary Wharf London, E14 5LQ

Telephone Orders
020 7038 8370 / 079 7055 0865

Email Orders
handbooks@sterlinglibs.com

Please send me the following books, disks or reports.

TICK	BOOK TITLE	PRICE (£)
☐	Work Experience in Accountancy - Workbook	£45.95
☐	The Accounts Assistant Job Manual – How to do the regular day to day tasks of an accounts assistant in Sage 50.	£65.95
☐	Month-End Accounting procedures	£40.95
☐	The Trainee Accountant – How to have a successful accounting career	£24.95
☐	Get your VAT return done in 5 steps	£25.95
☐	Business Intelligence – Start, Build & Run your own business and become financially independent.	£20.95
☐	Management Accounting practical guide	£45.95
☐	The Way to Get an Accounting Job in the UK - The 5 strategic steps	£22.95

PLEASE SEND MORE INFORMATION ON:

☐ Speaking/Seminars & accounting job fairs   ☐ Consulting & mentoring

YOUR DETAILS – FOR US TO SEND YOU THE BOOK(S) YOU'VE ORDERED

Name:

Address:

City/Town: Postcode:

Contact No.:   Email:

POSTAGE & PACKAGING OF £5 APPLY IF WITHIN UK AND £9 FOR INTERNATIONAL ORDERS

STERLING LIBS
CHARTERED ACCOUNTANT

QUICK ORDER FORM

Postal Orders
Sterling Libs Books,
Level 33, 25 Canada Square,
Canary Wharf London, E14 5LQ

Telephone Orders
020 7038 8370 / 079 7055 0865

Email Orders
handbooks@sterlinglibs.com

Please send me the following books, disks or reports.

TICK	BOOK TITLE	PRICE (£)
☐	Work Experience in Accountancy - Workbook	£45.95
☐	The Accounts Assistant Job Manual – How to do the regular day to day tasks of an accounts assistant in Sage 50.	£65.95
☐	Month-End Accounting procedures	£40.95
☐	The Trainee Accountant – How to have a successful accounting career	£24.95
☐	Get your VAT return done in 5 steps	£25.95
☐	Business Intelligence – Start, Build & Run your own business and become financially independent.	£20.95
☐	Management Accounting practical guide	£45.95
☐	The Way to Get an Accounting Job in the UK - The 5 strategic steps	£22.95

PLEASE SEND MORE INFORMATION ON:

☐ Speaking/Seminars & accounting job fairs   ☐ Consulting & mentoring

YOUR DETAILS – FOR US TO SEND YOU THE BOOK(S) YOU'VE ORDERED

Name:

Address:

City/Town: Postcode:

Contact No.:   Email:

POSTAGE & PACKAGING OF £5 APPLY IF WITHIN UK AND £9 FOR INTERNATIONAL ORDERS

Made in the USA
Charleston, SC
07 January 2017